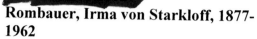

ALL ABOUT
PARTY FOODS & DRINKS

Joy of Cooking

ALL ABOUT
PARTY FOODS & DRINKS

IRMA S. ROMBAUER
MARION ROMBAUER BECKER
ETHAN BECKER

PHOTOGRAPHY BY TUCKER & HOSSLER

SCRIBNER
NEW YORK · LONDON · TORONTO · SYDNEY · SINGAPORE

SCRIBNER
1230 Avenue of the Americas
New York, NY 10020

WELDON OWEN INC.
Chief Executive Officer: John Owen
President: Terry Newell
Chief Operating Officer: Larry Partington
Vice President, International Sales: Stuart Laurence
Publisher: Roger Shaw
Creative Director: Gaye Allen
Associate Publisher: Val Cipollone
Associate Editor: Anna Mantzaris
Consulting Editors: Judith Dunham,
Barbara Ottenhoff
Art Director: Catherine Jacobes
Designer: Sarah Gifford
Photo Editor: Lisa Lee
Production Manager: Chris Hemesath
Shipping and Production Coordinator: Libby Temple
Production: Joan Olson
Food Stylist: Dan Becker
Food Styling Assistant: Jill Freed
Step-by-Step Photographer: Mike Falconer
Step-by-Step Food Stylist: Andrea Lucich

Joy of Cooking All About series was designed
and produced by Weldon Owen Inc.,
814 Montgomery Street, San Francisco,
California 94133

Set in Joanna MT and Gill Sans

Separations by Bright Arts Singapore
Printed in Singapore by Tien Wah Press (Pte.) Ltd.

10 9 8 7 6 5 4 3 2 1

Library of Congress Cataloging-in-Publication Data
is available.

ISBN 0-7432-1679-2

Recipe shown on half-title page: *New Potatoes Stuffed with
Sour Cream and Caviar*, 53
Recipe shown on title page: *Melon and Figs Wrapped in Prosciutto*, 48

CONTENTS

6 FOREWORD

8 ABOUT **PARTY FOODS**

13 ABOUT **CHIPS, CRACKERS & SANDWICHES**

23 ABOUT **DIPS & SPREADS**

39 ABOUT **CHEESE** PARTY FOODS

47 ABOUT **FRUIT & VEGETABLE** PARTY FOODS

57 ABOUT **PASTRY** PARTY FOODS

75 ABOUT **SEAFOOD** PARTY FOODS

85 ABOUT **CHICKEN** PARTY FOODS

93 ABOUT **MEAT** PARTY FOODS

107 ABOUT **PARTY DRINKS**

126 INDEX

128 ACKNOWLEDGMENTS

FOREWORD

"When you are entertaining, try not to feel that something unusual is expected of you. It isn't. Just be yourself," wrote my Granny Rom and Mom in an early edition of the Joy of Cooking. *With that reassuring advice, they set forth an approach to parties that has always served me well. I try to make a good impression with the party foods, little dishes, and drinks that I offer my guests. But I always make sure not to be too ambitious and to concentrate on recipes that I feel comfortable making and my guests will enjoy.*

Throughout this volume in the All About *series, you'll find a wide range of recipes that are as easy to make and serve for parties as they are delicious to eat. Accompanying them are tips and hints, step-by-step demonstrations, and serving suggestions that will help you achieve the goal of all hosts and hostesses: a party that will let you relax and just be yourself.*

You might notice that this collection of kitchen-tested recipes is adapted from the latest edition of the Joy of Cooking. *Just as our family has done for generations, we have worked to make this version of* Joy *a little bit better than the last. As a result, you'll find that some notes, recipes, and techniques have been changed to improve their clarity and usefulness. Since 1931, the* Joy of Cooking *has constantly evolved. And now, the* All About *series has taken* Joy *to a whole new stage, as you will see from the beautiful color photographs of finished dishes and clearly illustrated instructions for preparing and serving them. Granny Rom and Mom would have been delighted.*

I'm sure you'll find All About Party Foods & Drinks *to be both a useful and an enduring companion in your kitchen.*

Enjoy!

Ethan Becker pictured with his grandmother, Irma von Starkloff Rombauer (left), and his mother, Marion Rombauer Becker (right). Irma Rombauer published the first Joy of Cooking *at her own expense in 1931. Marion Rombauer Becker became coauthor in 1951.* Joy *as it has progressed through the decades (from top left to bottom right): the 1931 edition with Marion's depiction of St. Martha of Bethany, said to be the patron saint of cooking, "slaying the dragon of kitchen drudgery"; the 1943 edition; the 1951 edition; the 1962 edition; the 1975 edition; and the 1997 edition.*

About Party Foods

Party foods can be dips, spreads, pastries, olives, or nuts; they can be based on eggs, fruits, cheese, meats, vegetables, seafood, or breads. Canapés are a specific type of party food consisting of a thin bread, cracker, or pastry base, a spread, one or more toppings, and a garnish—in effect, tiny open-faced sandwiches. Indeed, the concept of party foods continues to broaden and now commonly includes little dishes— savory international fare that, by definition, is served in small or bite-sized portions. Generally speaking, almost anything served in portions that can be eaten with the fingers will qualify as party food. They may be served hot, at room temperature, or cold.

The selection of party foods in this book spans the globe, from classic American appetizers and Mexican *antojitos* ("little cravings") to recipes from the Scandinavian smorgasbord and *samosas*, the most popular small dishes of India. From Italy come the dishes that are most familiar to us in the form of the antipasto, which means simply "before the meal." Antipasti can be as simple and easy to make as *Melon and Figs Wrapped in Prosciutto*, 48, and *Bocconcini*, 40, cubes of fresh mozzarella marinated in olive oil, herbs, and spices. The French table contributes the assortment of raw vegetables called *Crudités*, 50, and their various accompaniments, *Gougères*, 59, elegant, small cheese puffs, and other signature party foods and *petits plats*.

Spanish cuisine offers *tapas*, the little dishes traditionally enjoyed with sherry. Small plates come from Greek, Turkish, and Middle Eastern cuisines, too, and are called *meze* or *mezethes*. This wide array includes ever-popular *Hummus*, 30, and *Baba Ghanoush*, 30, dips that are eaten on triangles of pita bread, and *Stuffed Grape Leaves*, 105.

Japanese cuisine is renowned for its spare, refined presentation and its full appreciation of each individual ingredient in a recipe. These qualities are evident in such small dishes as *Chicken Dumplings*, 91, and *Beef and Scallion Rolls*, 94. *Chinese Dumplings*, 72, are a fine example of *dim sum*, the little dishes favored by the Cantonese. Dim sum literally means "dot the heart," a phrase we have always thought implied small, pointed pleasures.

In choosing party foods to precede a dinner party or to serve at a gathering that will take the place of dinner, feel free to travel the globe. Just be sure to plan your selection with the whole menu in mind, striking a balance between tastes and textures and degrees of richness.

Entertaining

Since the first caveman invited a neighbor to share a haunch of roasted mastodon, there have been hosts and guests. The relationship is a natural and mutually satisfactory one, and over the centuries, human society has made an art out of "having people over"—whether that means offering a hungry traveler a bowl of soup or staging a wedding banquet for a thousand of one's daughter's closest friends. Entertaining guests is an act of friendship and an expression of generosity. It is perhaps our oldest social ritual, and our most universal—but, like everything else, it has changed with the times.

The elaborate entertaining of the past—developed when even middle-class families had servants and heirloom troves of silverware and good china—no longer seems to have much of a place in daily life. As the twenty-first century unfolds, in fact, we're convinced that the two most important elements of successful entertaining are simplicity and creativity. In short, to entertain well, be yourself. Offer your guests the things you both like and can manage well. Do this with a little imagination and a sense of style, remember a few basic rules, and you'll be an excellent host.

RULES FOR ENTERTAINING

- Don't overdo it. Nothing is more disconcerting to a guest than the impression that his or her presence is causing a household commotion. Confine all noticeable efforts to the period preceding your guests' arrival.

- Be prepared but be flexible. Satisfy yourself that you have anticipated every possible emergency—the howling child, your mate's exuberance, your helper's ineptness, your own last-minute qualms—and then relax and enjoy your guests.

- If, at the last minute, something does happen to upset your well-laid plans, rise to the occasion. A minor catastrophe could be the making of your party. Remember that the poet Horace once observed that "a host is like a general; it takes a mishap to reveal his genius."

- Select friends you think will genuinely enjoy one another, whether or not they've ever met.

- Written invitations are always preferable, but the telephone is far more common today and is perfectly acceptable.

- Invitations to a party should go out two to three weeks in advance; for a party on or near a major holiday, send invitations at least a month ahead of time.

- Remember these two important rules: Choose food that can be prepared ahead of time, so that you can spend more time at the table than over the stove, and never, ever, make a dish for company that you haven't made before and mastered.

Cocktail Parties

The cocktail party is an estimable but endangered social institution. Its demise may be blamed on factors as various as the waning popularity of hard liquor, the regrettable decline of the sibling arts of conversation and flirtation, and the growing acceptance in this country of the European idea that dinner by itself is sufficient diversion for an evening. (The cocktail party, remember, is an American invention.) We steadfastly defend the cocktail party, however, both as an abstract notion and as an uncomplicated and extremely pleasant means of entertaining. It offers a way to enjoy the company of family and friends that is different from serving a sit-down meal. Hosting a cocktail party is also an excellent means of entertaining business associates and professional contacts.

A good cocktail party begins with good liquors (and wines and beers if you like); "house" brands reflect on the quality of the house. Unless you plan to hire a professional bartender or the number of guests is so small that you or a volunteer guest can handle mixology duties without missing the fun, it's best to serve just one type of cocktail, made up in batches—pitchers of martinis or margaritas, for example. Or simply display exemplars of the four "basic" liquors (Scotch, bourbon, gin, and vodka) with an assortment of appropriate mixes, a bucket of ice, glasses in several sizes, and a long-handled bar spoon, and let guests serve themselves highballs and "rocks" drinks. Mixes aside, there should always be something nonalcoholic available; sparkling mineral water is practically de rigueur these days, and freshly squeezed orange juice is never out of place.

There must always be food at a cocktail party, of course, or the cocktails will quickly overwhelm the party. The food offered need not be complicated, nor even homemade. Pâtés and terrines purchased from a specialty food shop or an assortment of well-chosen cheeses, in either case served with crackers or sliced breads of good quality, are sufficient for an informal gathering. More sophisticated cocktail parties call for elegant party foods or, perhaps, an attractive service of smoked salmon or even caviar. In general, cocktail parties shouldn't last more than two hours, and those two hours should be found somewhere between 5 and 8 p.m.—never later, unless enough food is being served to constitute a light dinner. A shorter cocktail period is appropriate if it is a prelude to another event—a dinner out with the same guests, for instance, or an expedition to the theater. In this case, keep both drinks and food as simple as possible. For example, chilled Champagne and smoked salmon with black bread would be perfect.

The Open House

A variation on the cocktail party, usually specific to the year-end holidays, is the open house. The same basic rules apply, but such an event may run for three to four hours or even more, with the expectation that guests will drop by at their convenience during that period of time but rarely stay more than an hour or so. Keep in mind that this means of entertaining is particularly appropriate for busy holiday weekends, for which guests may be expected to have several invitations; it also permits the host to invite a larger number of people than might fit comfortably in the available quarters at one time. Because of the inevitable ebb and flow of guests, passed finger foods are inappropriate to an open house of any size and duration, and food tends to be rather more substantial than at a simple cocktail party. A modified buffet table is more appropriate, probably involving nothing that needs to be kept warm; baked ham, turkey, and a whole poached salmon make attractive and satisfying centerpieces for the array.

Planning Food for a Party

Before a dinner party, two or three kinds of party foods of the lighter variety are usually sufficient; you want to stimulate guests' appetites, not sate them. For a cocktail party without dinner to follow, prepare five or six different party foods, including some more substantial fare. For a reception or party that will take the place of dinner, serve six to eight party foods with lots of variety and with heartier kinds added. As a general rule, figure two pieces per person of each. (These loose guidelines do not include dips, which may always be included.) Whether setting out a buffet table laden with party foods or passing trays of bite-sized morsels, vary the shapes, sizes, colors, and textures to make the selections visually enticing.

Party foods can often be prepared ahead of time and refrigerated, or in a few cases even frozen, for future use. Party fare made with pastry, 57 to 73, are especially convenient.

It is usually best to choose party foods that don't require last-minute cooking, so that you can spend some time with your guests. If you are serving hot party foods, pass them after all of your guests have arrived so that everyone has the opportunity to taste them.

Menus for Entertaining

OPEN HOUSE
Turkey Biscuits with Chutney
    Butter, 17
Tortilla Española, 54
Lemon Rosemary Chicken on
    Skewers, 87
Food Processor Cheese Straws, 60

CELEBRATION
Brie Baked in Pastry, 42
Salmon Mousse, 34
New Potatoes Stuffed with Sour
    Cream and Caviar, 53
Parmesan Straws, 60
Sliced French Bread
Champagne Punch, 122

ASIAN
Chinese Dumplings, 72
Vietnamese Summer Rolls, 82
Baby Riblets, 99
Beef Satay with Peanut Sauce, 94

MIDDLE EASTERN
Hummus, 30
Baba Ghanoush, 30
Herbed Laban, 43
Barbecued Kebabs, 97
Pita Bread

SOUTH-OF-THE-BORDER
Tortilla Chips, 15
Black-Bean Salsa Dip, 25
Salsa Fresca, 28
Salsa Verde Cruda, 28
Guacamole, 29
Masa Boats with Assorted Toppings, 69
Margaritas, 118

RUSSIAN
Smoked Salmon and Egg
    Sandwiches, 18
Eggplant Caviar, 33
Mushroom Triangles, 62
Pirozhki, 66

ABOUT
CHIPS,
CRACKERS &
SANDWICHES

Crisp potato chips, crunchy crackers, and simple sandwiches are indispensable party foods. They're the perfect addition to the entertaining table.

Chips, crackers, biscuits, and breads are easy to dress up. The fresher and better the ingredients used, the better the result. Guests will appreciate homemade versions of party favorites like potato and tortilla chips.

If you are making a lot of sandwiches for a party, you can save time by arranging the ingredients like an assembly line. Begin by lining up the bread in rows, pairing the slices so they will match. To facilitate assembly, make sure the dressing (especially if it is butter) is soft enough to spread. Add the filling and then put the bread slices together and press gently. When cutting the completed sandwiches, use a very sharp knife to avoid squashing them or creating ragged edges.

Root Chips, 15

Potato or Saratoga Chips

4 servings

Properly fried chips are light, without any greasy feel. It helps to use a deep-fat fryer with a basket. Do not let the chips brown too quickly, or they'll be limp once removed from the fat. It should take them about 3 minutes to turn from white to gold. Since many conditions affect how rapidly anything cooks and browns, adjust the tempera- ture to get the timing right on the first few, then continue with the rest.

Soak in cold water for 2 hours, changing the water twice:

1 pound baking potatoes, peeled and sliced as thinly as possible

Drain and dry very well between clean dish towels. Heat in a deep fryer or deep, heavy pot to 380°F:

3 inches vegetable or olive oil

Slowly drop a handful of potatoes into the oil. Poke them several times with a spoon or a chopstick so they don't stick to one another. Cook until golden, 2 to 3 minutes. Remove to paper towels to drain. Sprinkle, if desired, with:

Salt to taste

HOW TO CUT POTATOES FOR POTATO CHIPS

When it comes to thinly slicing potatoes for potato chips, the cook can use either a sharp knife or a mandoline. While the former is a completely respectable choice, the latter can be a lot of fun. You can leave the skin on or peel it from the potato.

1 To slice potatoes using a sharp knife, start by slicing a thin piece from the side of the potato. This keeps the potato steady when slicing.

2 Set the potato cut side down on a cutting board. Slice the potato as thinly as possible. Generally speaking, the thinner the knife, the thinner the slices will be.

3 To slice potatoes using a mandoline, follow the manufacturer's instructions. Choose the setting that produces the thinnest slice, secure the potato, and begin slicing. Keep your fingers well away from the cutting blade.

4 For waffled potato chips, use the waffle-cut attachment on the mandoline.

Tortilla Chips

48 chips

Homemade tortilla chips based on top-quality store-bought or homemade corn tortillas are a real treat and amazingly easy to make. Corn tortillas have more flavor than flour tortillas. Serve these homemade chips with Black-Bean Salsa Dip, 25, Salsa Verde Cruda, 28, or Mango Salsa, 29.

Quarter:

12 corn tortillas

Heat in a medium skillet to 375°F:

2 cups vegetable oil

Add as many tortilla quarters as will fit in a single layer and fry, turning once, until browned and crisp. Remove to paper towels to drain. Repeat with the remaining tortillas. Sprinkle immediately with:

Salt to taste

Root Chips

6 servings

Though the potato crisps most successfully, other root vegetables can also be turned into chips, providing varied flavors and colors. When shopping for root vegetables, avoid overly large specimens, which can have tough or woody cores. Choose those that are the heaviest for their size.

With a sharp knife, vegetable peeler, or food processor, peel, then slice as thinly as possible (at most ⅛ inch thick) any combination of the following, about 1½ pounds total:

Baking potatoes
Celery root
Carrots
Parsnips
Rutabagas
Sweet potatoes
Red or golden beets

Place the potatoes, celery root, parsnips, and rutabagas in cold water after slicing to prevent discoloring. Heat in a deep fryer or deep, heavy pot to 370° to 380°F:

2 inches vegetable oil

Drain the vegetables and pat them dry. Fry each type of vegetable separately, adding just a few at a time so as not to overcrowd. Poke the slices with a spoon or a chopstick to prevent them from sticking. Cook until golden brown. The time will vary slightly for each individual vegetable. Remove to paper towels to drain. Season with:

Salt to taste

Serve hot.

Nachos

10 to 12 servings

Nachos were apparently invented by, and named for, Ignacio "Nacho" Anaya at a restaurant called the Victory Club in the Mexican border town of Piedras Negras (just across the Rio Grande from Eagle Pass, Texas) in 1946 or 1947. The original "Nacho's Special" was nothing more than fried tortilla chips topped with cheese and sliced jalapeños. These nachos (right) are slightly more complicated than Nacho's original, but they're addictively good. There are many types of canned chili peppers available, from mild to fiery, so choose carefully.

Preheat the broiler.

On an 11- or 12-inch round heatproof platter, spread (they can be slightly overlapping):

4 ounces tortilla chips (about 4 cups)

Sprinkle with:

1½ cups grated sharp Cheddar cheese
1½ cups grated Monterey Jack cheese
One 4-ounce can chopped mild green chili peppers, drained

Broil 5 to 6 inches from the heat until the cheese is melted, 2 to 3 minutes. Top with your choice of:

Sour cream
Sliced pitted black olives
Chopped scallions
Chopped jalapeño pepper rings
Chopped fresh cilantro

Serve immediately.

Lemon Crackers

About 44 crackers

The dough for the crackers can be shaped into a log, wrapped tightly, and frozen up to 2 months. The day before baking, thaw the log in the refrigerator, then slice and bake just before company arrives.

Whisk together in a bowl:

**1½ cups finely grated Parmesan
    cheese**

¾ cup all-purpose flour

1 teaspoon finely grated lemon zest

**¾ teaspoon coarsely ground black
    pepper**

Add and cut in with 2 knives or a pastry blender until the mixture resembles coarse crumbs:

**4 tablespoons (½ stick) cold
    butter, cut into small pieces**

Make a well in the center and add:

1½ tablespoons water

1 teaspoon fresh lemon juice

Stir with a fork just until the mixture forms a dough. Briefly knead the dough just until combined. Transfer to a sheet of wax paper and, using the wax paper as an aid, shape it into a squared-off log, about 11 inches long. Wrap in the wax paper and refrigerate until firm enough to slice, about 1 hour. (The dough can be prepared up to this point 2 days in advance.) Preheat the oven to 375°F. Cut the dough into ¼-inch-thick slices and arrange 1 inch apart on baking sheets. Bake one sheet at a time until the crackers are golden around the edges, about 10 minutes. Transfer carefully with a spatula to a rack and let cool completely. Sprinkle with:

Coarsely ground black pepper

MAKING BASIC CRACKERS

Almost any bread dough may be turned into crackers. Simply roll the dough out ⅛ inch thick, cut crackers to the desired size and shape, and place about 1 inch apart on a lightly greased baking sheet. You can brush the tops with melted butter or beaten egg and sprinkle sesame, poppy, or any favorite seeds on top before cutting. For crisp crackers, use a dough such as basic pizza dough, although any lean bread dough will do. For richer, more buttery crackers, do the same with brioche dough. Experiment with different types of dough to find your favorite. Bake the crackers on the baking sheet in a preheated 450°F oven until they begin to turn light or golden brown, 6 to 9 minutes.

Ham Biscuits

About 24 biscuits

This popular southern treat can be served already assembled, or you can let guests put together their own.

Preheat the oven to 425°F.

Prepare the dough for:

Basic Rolled Biscuits, opposite

adding:

**¼ cup snipped fresh chives
    (optional)**

Roll out the dough into a circle or rectangle about ¾ inch thick. Cut into 2-inch rounds, hearts, or diamonds with a biscuit or cookie cutter. Place 1 inch apart on ungreased baking sheets and brush the tops with:

Melted butter

Bake until golden on top, about 15 minutes. Meanwhile, for honey mustard, whisk together in a small bowl:

½ cup whole-grain mustard

2 tablespoons honey, or to taste

1 tablespoon Dijon mustard

Or have ready for spreading:

4 tablespoons (½ stick) butter

When the biscuits are cool enough to handle, split them, spread with the honey mustard or butter, and make sandwiches with:

**12 ounces thinly sliced smoked or
    baked ham or prosciutto**

Serve warm or at room temperature.

Turkey Biscuits with Chutney Butter

About 24 biscuits

Any flavored butter can be substituted for the chutney butter in these biscuits.
Prepare the dough for:
Basic Rolled Biscuits, below
While the biscuits are baking, stir together:
8 tablespoons (1 stick) butter, softened
3 tablespoons mango chutney
Pinch of curry powder
Pinch of salt

When the biscuits are cool enough to handle, split them, spread with the chutney butter, and make sandwiches with:
12 ounces sliced turkey breast
Serve warm or at room temperature, or to serve the assembled biscuits hot, heat on a baking sheet in a 350°F oven until warmed through, about 10 minutes.

Basic Rolled Biscuits

About twenty-four 2-inch biscuits

Position a rack in the center of the oven. Preheat the oven to 450°F. Have ready a large ungreased baking sheet.
Whisk together thoroughly in a large bowl:
2 cups all-purpose flour
2½ teaspoons baking powder
½ to ¾ teaspoon salt
Drop in:
5 to 6 tablespoons cold unsalted butter, cut into pieces
Cut in the butter with 2 knives or a pastry blender, tossing the pieces with the flour mixture to coat and separate them as you work. For biscuits with crunchy edges and a flaky, layered structure, continue to cut in the butter until the largest pieces are the size of peas and the rest resemble breadcrumbs. For classic fluffy biscuits, continue to cut in the butter until the mixture resembles coarse breadcrumbs. Do not allow the butter to melt or form a paste with the flour. Add all at once:

¾ cup milk
Mix with a rubber spatula, wooden spoon, or fork just until most of the dry ingredients are moistened. With a lightly floured hand, gather the dough into a ball and knead it gently against the sides and bottom of the bowl 5 to 10 times, turning and pressing any loose pieces into the dough each time until they adhere and the bowl is fairly clean.
TO SHAPE ROUND BISCUITS: Transfer the dough to a lightly floured surface. With a lightly floured rolling pin or your fingers, roll out or pat the dough ½ inch thick. Cut out 1¾- to 2-inch rounds with a drinking glass or biscuit cutter dipped in flour; push the cutter straight down into the dough and pull it out without twisting for biscuits that will rise evenly. You can reroll the scraps and cut additional biscuits (they are never as tender as the first-cut).
TO SHAPE SQUARE BISCUITS: Roll out the dough ½ inch thick (¼ to ⅜ inch if cooking on a griddle) into a

square or rectangle. Trim a fraction of an inch from the edges of the dough with a sharp knife before cutting into 2-inch squares.
TO BAKE BISCUITS IN THE OVEN: For browner tops, you can brush the biscuit tops with:
Milk or melted butter
Place the biscuits on a baking sheet at least 1 inch apart for biscuits with crusty sides or close together for biscuits that are joined and remain soft on the sides. Bake until the biscuits are golden brown on the top and a deeper golden brown on the bottom, 10 to 12 minutes. Serve hot.
TO COOK BISCUITS ON A GRIDDLE: To avoid completely charring the outside before the inside is cooked, roll out the biscuit dough just ¼ to ⅜ inch thick. Cook at least 1 inch apart on a lightly greased, medium-hot griddle until brown on one side, 3 to 4 minutes; turn and cook until brown on the other side and cooked in the center. Serve hot.

Griddle-Baked Quesadillas

6 appetizer servings

These delicious tortilla snacks can be stuffed with all kinds of Mexican flavors, from melting cheese and the traditional herb epazote to slivers of cooked meat, fish, or poultry. Here, a simple combination of cheese with roasted peppers and fried onions is baked in your choice of flour or corn tortillas.

Heat in a medium skillet over medium heat until hot:

1½ teaspoons vegetable oil

Add and cook until nicely browned, about 8 minutes:

1 small white onion, halved and thinly sliced

Stir in:

1½ cups roasted pepper strips, such as fresh poblano or Anaheim peppers, canned green chili peppers, or bottled roasted peppers

¼ teaspoon salt, or to taste

Heat through, then remove from the heat. Have ready:

2 cups grated Mexican Chihuahua, Monterey Jack, or brick cheese

6 flour tortillas or very fresh corn tortillas

Lightly oil a griddle and heat over medium heat. Place as many tortillas as will fit in a single layer on the hot griddle. Top each with ⅓ cup of the cheese and about 2 tablespoons of the roasted pepper mixture. Bake on the griddle until the cheese begins to melt, about 1 minute, then fold the tortillas in half. Continue griddle-baking until crispy on both sides, another minute or two. Cut into wedges (opposite) and serve immediately, accompanied with:

Salsa Fresca, 28, or Guacamole, 29

STOVE-ROASTING PEPPERS

Roasting provides the best way to remove the skin of peppers. This is the simplest method for roasting fresh and dried peppers. Place whole peppers directly in the flames of your gas burner on its highest setting. (If you do not have a gas burner, set the peppers on a grill called an asador, one that rests above the burner.) Keep an eye on the peppers and turn them frequently with tongs, letting the peppers blister or char. Continue until the entire surface is blistered. Many cooks stove-roast dried chili peppers before rehydrating them, to deepen the flavors.

Danish Shrimp Sandwiches

8 small open-faced sandwiches

These finger sandwiches are often part of a Scandinavian smorgasbord.

Lay on a work surface:

4 thick slices light rye or white bread

Spread generously with:

Unsalted butter, softened

Cover each bread slice with:

About 25 tiny bay shrimp, well drained

Sprinkle generously with:

Ground black pepper

Cut in half and serve with:

Lemon wedges for squeezing

Danish Beef Sandwiches

8 small open-faced sandwiches

Combine well:

About 1 cup minced cold roast beef

⅓ cup mayonnaise, or to taste

Salt and ground black pepper to taste

Lay on a work surface:

4 slices dark bread

Spread generously with:

Unsalted butter, softened

Top each with one-quarter of the beef mixture and sprinkle each with:

1 tablespoon minced red onion

1 tablespoon sweet pickle relish

Cut in half and serve.

Smoked Salmon and Egg Sandwiches

8 small open-faced sandwiches

Lay on a work surface:

4 thin slices dark rye bread

Spread generously with:

Unsalted butter, softened

Divide among the bread slices:

4 large slices smoked salmon (about 4 ounces total)

Lay diagonally in a strip across each piece of bread:

About ¼ cup firm scrambled eggs, at room temperature

Sprinkle with:

Snipped fresh dill

Cut in half and serve.

Bruschetta

From the Italian word meaning "roasted over coals," bruschetta is the original garlic bread. In its simplest form, it is nothing more than grilled country bread rubbed with garlic cloves and brushed with olive oil. (The Tuscans call it *fett'unta*, meaning "under oil.") Bruschetta can also serve as the foundation for a wide variety of toppings, however. A single bruschetta makes a good appetizer, while two or three will make a nice lunch when accompanied with a simple salad. If you follow the same process with smaller pieces of bread, you will be making *crostini*, or little toasts, which are traditionally served as appetizers.

Bruschetta with Tomatoes and Basil

8 slices

Prepare a medium-hot charcoal fire or preheat the broiler.
Place on the grill or under the broiler:

8 thick slices crusty firm Italian bread or other country-style bread

Grill or broil, turning once, until golden brown, about 3 minutes each side. Remove from the heat and rub the surface with:

2 large cloves garlic, halved

Brush with:

3 to 4 tablespoons extra-virgin olive oil

Combine well:

4 medium, ripe tomatoes, cored and diced
½ cup slivered fresh basil leaves
Salt and ground black pepper to taste

Divide the tomato mixture among the grilled bread slices and serve immediately.

BRUSCHETTA WITH ASSORTED MEDITERRANEAN RELISHES

For an unusual and very tasty sandwich platter, make a large batch of bruschetta and top with several of the relishes below.

Grill or broil the bread, rub with garlic, and brush with oil as directed for *Bruschetta with Tomatoes and Basil, opposite.* Top each slice with about 2 tablespoons of *Tapenade, 32, Tuna Tapenade, 32, Taramasalata, 34, White Bean and Roasted Garlic Puree, 36,* or *Whipped Feta with Roasted Peppers, 36.*

BRUSCHETTA WITH PROSCIUTTO AND FRESH FIGS

There is nothing to trim on a fresh fig except the stem.

Grill or broil the bread, rub with garlic, and brush with oil as directed for *Bruschetta with Tomatoes and Basil, opposite.* Top each slice with 2 slices prosciutto and 1 fresh fig halved through the stem end.

BRUSCHETTA WITH GRILLED PORTOBELLO MUSHROOMS

Brush 4 large portobello mushroom caps with ¼ cup extra-virgin olive oil. Grill, gill side up, until cooked through, 8 to 10 minutes. Remove from the heat and halve. Grill or broil the bread, rub with garlic, and brush with oil as directed for *Bruschetta with Tomatoes and Basil, opposite.* Top each slice with a half mushroom and sprinkle with minced fresh rosemary or sage (about 2 tablespoons total).

BRUSCHETTA WITH MOZZARELLA AND FRESH OREGANO

Grill or broil the bread, rub with garlic, and brush with oil as directed for *Bruschetta with Tomatoes and Basil, opposite.* Top each slice with shredded mozzarella cheese (about 8 ounces total). Broil just until the cheese is bubbling. Top with diced fresh tomatoes (about 1 large tomato total) and chopped fresh oregano (about 2 tablespoons total).

Anchovy Toasts

16 slices

These little toasts are in the style of crostini, since the bread is cut from a narrow loaf. The toasts are the ideal size for eating with your fingers. The anchovies are tamed with a quick soak, then brightened with vinegar, garlic, and fresh parsley.

Soak for 10 minutes in cold water to cover:

4 ounces anchovies, drained

Drain, pat dry, and mince. Combine well with:

3 tablespoons extra-virgin olive oil
1 tablespoon red wine vinegar
3 tablespoons chopped fresh parsley
2 cloves garlic, minced
Ground black pepper to taste

Preheat the broiler.
Place on a baking sheet:

16 slices French bread, cut on a diagonal from a baguette or other narrow loaf

Broil until golden, about 3 minutes each side. Spread the toasts with the anchovy mixture and broil just until warm, about 1 minute. Serve the toasts immediately.

ABOUT
DIPS &
SPREADS

*D*ips have become a staple American party food. Quick and easy to prepare, they offer the opportunity for endless flavor combinations. Extremely versatile, dips can be built on a number of bases, including sour cream, crème fraîche, soft cheeses, mayonnaise, and cream cheese.

Spreads are a bit thicker than dips and usually feature ingredients with a more substantial texture, such as firm cheeses, cooked beans, or even pureed seafood, sometimes combined with the same smooth bases found in dips.

Richness of flavor and consistency is a characteristic dips and spreads share. To lower the fat content, use reduced-fat versions of the dairy products called for in the recipes on the following pages. Or opt for those recipes made primarily with vegetables or beans.

Clockwise from top: Guacamole, 29; Taramasalata, 34; Blue Cheese Spread with Walnuts, 36

Preparing and Serving Dips

Prepare cold dips at least 1 hour ahead of time or even a day in advance to allow the flavors to blend. Hot dips can be assembled ahead, covered, kept refrigerated until ready to cook, and they can be reheated in the microwave. Serve cold or room-temperature dips in small bowls, hollowed-out large round loaves of bread, or vegetable "containers," such as cabbage leaves, lettuce cups, or bell peppers. In warmer weather, be sure to place the dip container in a larger container of crushed ice when serving. Accompany dips with an assortment of cut-up raw vegetables and a selection of crackers, assorted breads, chips, seafood, or cubes of cheese or meat. Plan on about 1 cup dip to serve 4 people.

Red Onion Dip

About 2 cups

A great improvement on the standard onion dip.

Stir together in a large nonstick skillet over medium-high heat:

3 small red onions, finely chopped (about 2 cups)

2 cups beef stock

1½ tablespoons minced peeled fresh ginger

3 cloves garlic, minced

1 teaspoon fresh thyme leaves or minced fresh parsley, or scant ½ teaspoon dried

Salt and ground black pepper to taste

Bring to a boil, stirring, until almost all of the stock has been absorbed by the onion, about 15 minutes; watch it carefully at the end so that it doesn't burn. Remove to a bowl and stir in:

1 teaspoon balsamic vinegar

Let cool completely, then stir in:

1 cup sour cream

Serve slightly chilled.

Baked Artichoke Dip

About 2½ cups

Preheat the oven to 400°F.
Stir together in a medium bowl:

1 cup mayonnaise

1 cup grated Parmesan cheese

½ cup finely chopped onions

Pulse in a food processor until finely chopped:

One 13¾-ounce can artichoke hearts, well drained

Stir into the cheese mixture along with:

1 tablespoon fresh lemon juice or dry white wine

¼ to ½ teaspoon ground black pepper

Scrape into a small baking dish or ovenproof crock. Combine and sprinkle over the dip:

3 tablespoons dry unseasoned breadcrumbs

1 teaspoon olive oil

Bake until the top is browned, about 20 minutes. Serve with:

Crackers or toast

Hot Crab Dip

About 2 cups

Preheat the oven to 325°F. Butter a 2-cup ovenproof bowl.
Puree in a food processor until smooth:

8 ounces cream cheese, softened
¾ cup mayonnaise
2 tablespoons minced onions
1 teaspoon drained horseradish
1 teaspoon Worcestershire sauce
¼ teaspoon salt

Scrape into the bowl. Fold in, above:

**One 6-ounce can crabmeat,
   drained**

If desired, sprinkle with:

Slivered almonds

Bake until heated through, about 25 minutes. Serve with:

Crackers

Black-Bean Salsa Dip

About 1¼ cups

This no-fat dip can be served with Tortilla Chips, 15, or spooned into Masa Boats, 69, and garnished with any or all of the suggestions below.
Puree in a food processor until smooth:

**One 15½-ounce can black beans,
   rinsed and drained**
**6 tablespoons medium-hot or hot
   salsa**
1½ tablespoons fresh lime juice
1 small clove garlic, minced

Garnish with:

**Diced tomatoes, chopped fresh
   cilantro, and/or diced red bell
   peppers**

Serve with:

Tortilla chips

CANNED BEANS

Brands of canned beans vary in quality. Rinsing canned beans improves the taste a little and removes excess salt. To rinse well, put the beans in a large sieve set in a pot or bowl and let cold water run over the beans until the pot is filled, raking the beans with your fingers. Drain, repeat, and then drain well. For a full 2 cups cooked beans, you will need to start with a large can, 19 or 20 ounces. The smaller 15- or 16-ounce can holds only 1½ to 1¾ cups.

Spinach Yogurt Dip

About 2 cups

For a creamier consistency, drain the yogurt by placing it in a sieve lined with a clean dish towel or coffee filter for about 30 minutes.

Thaw, squeezing as dry as possible:

One 10-ounce package frozen chopped spinach

Mince in a food processor:

3 scallions, chopped

1 to 2 cloves garlic, chopped

Add the spinach along with:

2 cups low-fat yogurt, or 1 cup full-fat or low-fat yogurt and 1 cup nonfat cottage cheese

2 tablespoons grated Parmesan cheese

2 tablespoons sour cream (optional)

⅛ teaspoon freshly grated or ground nutmeg

Salt to taste

Pulse until smooth. Refrigerate for at least 1 hour or up to 24 hours. Serve in a bowl with:

Cut-up raw vegetables

Sliced bread

SPINACH YOGURT DIP IN A BREAD BOWL

Prepare Spinach Yogurt Dip, left, and refrigerate. Up to 1 hour before serving, make the bread bowl: Cut the top inch off a crusty round loaf of bread. Pull the bread out of the center to hollow it. Spoon the dip in and serve the removed bread chunks for dipping. Accompany with additional sliced bread and raw vegetables for dipping.

Seven-Layer Dip

About 20 servings

This substantial appetizer is best warm but can be served at room temperature. Assemble and serve it in a glass dish to display the brightly colored layers of vegetables and cheese. To increase the heat, replace the mild green chili peppers with minced fresh jalapeños.

Preheat the broiler.

In a 13 x 9-inch glass baking dish, evenly spread:

One 16-ounce can refried beans

Mash together and spread over the beans:

3 large ripe Hass avocados, peeled and pitted

3 tablespoons fresh lime juice

Mix together and spread over the avocado layer:

2 cups sour cream

1 envelope (1 ounce) taco seasoning

In the order listed, sprinkle with:

3 tablespoons drained chopped canned mild green chili peppers

One or two 5¾-ounce cans pitted black olives, drained and sliced

8 ripe plum tomatoes, chopped (about 4 cups)

2 cups grated sharp Cheddar cheese

Broil about 4 inches from the heat just until the cheese is melted, 1 to 2 minutes. If desired, sprinkle the top with:

Chopped fresh cilantro or scallions

Serve with:

Sturdy tortilla chips or toasted wedges of pita bread

AVOCADOS

Grown in southern California and Florida, avocados are available year-round. California specializes in the Hass, a purplish black, pebbly skinned avocado of the Guatemalan type. Hass avocados weigh about 8 ounces and have superior flavor. Their flesh is so rich and buttery because it contains twice as much fat as the smaller, smooth-skinned, green Mexican type of avocados grown in Florida. (California's other avocado, the smooth green Fuerte, is probably a Guatemalan-Mexican hybrid.) Although fat means calories, most fat in avocados is monounsaturated, the friendly sort found in olives.

Salsa Fresca

About 2 cups

This recipe for Mexican salsa is easily doubled or tripled, but try to make only as much as you will use immediately, as it loses its texture on standing and the chili peppers increase in heat. Regional variations include using scallions or white or red onions, water instead of lime juice, and in Yucatán, sour-orange juice instead of lime juice. Any sort of fresh chili pepper can be used—each contributes its distinctive character. Rinsing the chopped onions eliminates the biting aftertaste that could otherwise overwhelm the other ingredients. As you can see, precise amounts are less important than the happy marriage of flavors, so taste as you go. In American-style Mexican food, this type of salsa is sometimes called pico de gallo.

Combine in a medium bowl:

**½ small white or red onion or
    8 slender scallions, finely
    chopped, rinsed, and drained**

**2 tablespoons fresh lime juice or
    cold water**

Prepare the following ingredients, setting them aside, then add all together to the onion mixture:

**2 large ripe tomatoes, or 3 to
    5 ripe plum tomatoes, seeded,
    if desired, and finely diced**

**¼ to ½ cup chopped fresh cilantro
    (leaves and tender stems)**

**3 to 5 serrano or fresh jalapeño
    peppers, or ¼ to 1 habanero
    pepper, or to taste, seeded and
    minced**

6 radishes, finely diced (optional)

**1 medium clove garlic, minced
    (optional)**

Stir together well. Season with:

¼ teaspoon salt, or to taste

Serve immediately (above back).

Salsa Verde Cruda

About 2 cups

Intensely fresh, pungent, and herbal, this tomatillo salsa is the easiest salsa of all. It is especially good with fish, chicken, steamed or roasted vegetables, and eggs. However, since the onion is not rinsed and everything is whirled to a puree, it must be served within an hour of preparing for optimum quality. If left to sit, the raw onion will overpower the sauce.

Combine in a food processor or blender and coarsely puree, leaving the mixture a little chunky:

**8 ounces tomatillos, husked,
    rinsed, and coarsely chopped**

**1 small white or red onion,
    coarsely chopped**

**3 to 5 fresh green chili peppers
    (such as serrano or jalapeño),
    seeded and coarsely chopped**

1 clove garlic, peeled (optional)

**3 to 4 tablespoons fresh cilantro
    sprigs**

Remove to a medium bowl and stir in enough cold water to loosen the mixture to a saucelike consistency. Stir in:

1 teaspoon salt, or to taste

¾ teaspoon sugar (optional)

Serve immediately (above front).

Mango Salsa

About 3 cups

Use this as a master recipe for fruit salsas—wonderful with just about any food but particularly with grilled or sautéed fish. Papaya, pineapple, peaches, or apricots can be substituted for the mango; basil or parsley can stand in for the cilantro; and pineapple or guava juice is a good alternative to the orange juice.

Combine in a large bowl:

¼ cup fresh lime juice

1 small red onion, chopped, rinsed, and drained

Prepare the following ingredients, setting them aside, then add all together to the onion mixture:

1 large ripe mango, peeled, pitted, and coarsely chopped

1 small red bell pepper, cut into thin strips

¼ cup coarsely chopped fresh cilantro

1 clove garlic, minced

¼ cup fresh orange juice

1 fresh jalapeño or other small chili pepper, finely chopped

Stir together well. Season with:

Salt and cracked black peppercorns to taste

Serve immediately. This salsa will keep, covered and refrigerated, for up to 1 day.

Guacamole

About 2 cups

Use a large fork or a potato masher to gently crush ripe avocados into this classic Mexican avocado relish (below). Serve guacamole as an accompaniment to tacos, tortilla chips, cut-up raw vegetables (such as jícama, cucumber, and radish slices), and grilled fish or poultry.

Using the coarsest side of a four-sided grater, grate into a medium bowl:

½ small white onion

1 or 2 fresh jalapeño peppers, or to taste

1 medium, firm, ripe tomato

Using a large knife, halve:

2 large or 3 medium, ripe avocados, preferably Hass

Remove the avocado pits, then use a large spoon to scoop the flesh into the bowl with the onion mixture. Use a large fork or potato masher to coarsely mash the avocados together with the onion mixture. Stir in:

2 tablespoons chopped fresh cilantro

1 tablespoon fresh lime juice

½ teaspoon salt, or to taste

Cover with plastic wrap placed directly on the surface of the mixture and let stand for a few minutes. Serve garnished with:

Fresh cilantro sprigs

Hummus (Middle Eastern Chickpea and Sesame Dip)

About 2 cups

If using canned chickpeas, rinse 2 cups (one 16-ounce can) and puree as directed, using water to thin the puree. In Egypt, hummus (opposite) is flavored with cumin; use ½ teaspoon ground cumin for this quantity.

Rinse, then soak 8 to 12 hours:

¾ cup dried chickpeas

Drain and place in a pan with water to cover by 2 inches. Bring to a boil, reduce the heat, and simmer until very tender, about 1½ hours. Drain, reserving the cooking liquid. Remove the chickpeas to a food processor or blender and add:

⅓ cup fresh lemon juice
3 tablespoons tahini
2 cloves garlic, finely minced
Salt to taste

Puree until smooth, adding 2 to 3 tablespoons of the cooking liquid as needed to obtain a soft, creamy consistency. Remove to a shallow serving bowl and garnish with:

1 tablespoon olive oil
1 tablespoon finely chopped fresh parsley
Sprinkling of hot or sweet paprika

Serve with:

Warm pita bread

CHICKPEAS

Chickpeas seem indestructible. They come out of a can firmer than other beans, hold up well in stews and salads, and can withstand grinding to make falafel or baking for a pop-in-your-mouth snack. They are also known as garbanzos and ceci beans. Chickpeas are a constant in Mediterranean cuisines, from Middle Eastern hummus to Moroccan couscous, imparting a mild nutty flavor to all.

Herb Dip

About 1½ cups

Try this Middle Eastern–inspired dip with crisp snow peas and radishes. Other mild fresh green herbs can be substituted or combined with the parsley for a variety of herb dips. Try basil in equal quantity or a lesser amount of dill, thyme, or marjoram.

Pulse in a food processor until chopped:

3 scallions, trimmed
½ bunch fresh flat-leaf parsley, large stems trimmed

Transfer to a medium bowl and stir in:

¾ cup mayonnaise
¼ cup sour cream
1 tablespoon fresh lemon juice
1 tablespoon ground cumin

Serve with:

Crudités, 50, or crackers

Baba Ghanoush (Roasted Eggplant Dip)

About 2 cups

In Greece, when friends gather in tavernas or ouzerís to socialize over glasses of potent anise-flavored ouzo or resinated wine, the table is always cluttered with plates full of little snacks called mezethes. *These might include a creamy feta cheese dip, a baba ghanoush, or the pureed fish roe known as* taramasalata—*all to be eaten on triangles of pita bread—or such items as stuffed grape leaves or assorted phyllo pastries stuffed with olives, greens, or cheese. You can stir ½ cup yogurt into the eggplant puree just before serving, then garnish.*

Preheat the oven to 400°F.

Pierce in several places:

3 medium eggplants (about 4 pounds)

Roast on a baking sheet until the skins are dark mahogany in color and the flesh feels soft, 45 to 60 minutes. Let stand until cool enough to handle. Split the eggplants and scoop the flesh into a colander. Press lightly to extract the excess liquid. Remove to a food processor and add:

1½ tablespoons tahini
2 cloves garlic, chopped
Juice of 1 large lemon
½ teaspoon salt

Pulse until smooth. Taste and adjust the seasonings. Remove to a shallow serving bowl and garnish with:

1 tablespoon olive oil
1 tablespoon finely chopped fresh parsley
Several pitted black olives (optional)

Serve with:

Warm pita bread

Tapenade (Caper Olive Paste)

About 2¾ cups

Based on its name, the one essential ingredient in this popular spread is the caper—called tapeno *in Provence. Tapenade made without capers or with only a hint of them is sometimes called* olivade.

Combine in a food processor:

2 cups black olives, preferably oil cured, pitted

3 anchovies, rinsed and patted dry (optional)
3 tablespoons drained capers
3 tablespoons extra-virgin olive oil
2 tablespoons brandy or fresh lemon juice
2 cloves garlic, coarsely chopped
2 teaspoons fresh thyme leaves, or 1 teaspoon dried

Salt and ground black pepper to taste

Pulse until the mixture is still coarse but of a uniform consistency. Serve with:

Crusty French bread or Crudités, 50

Tuna Tapenade

About 1 cup

With a fork, flake and transfer to a food processor:

One 6-ounce can tuna packed in olive oil, drained (if tuna packed in olive oil is not available, use white tuna packed in water, drained)

Add:

4 tablespoons (½ stick) unsalted butter, softened
1 cup best-quality green olives (such as Picholine), pitted

¼ cup minced fresh basil
Grated zest of 1 lemon
2 tablespoons fresh lemon juice

Process just until blended; the mixture should remain slightly coarse. If desired, season with:

Ground black pepper to taste

Transfer to a medium bowl and serve at room temperature. The tapenade can be stored, covered and refrigerated, for up to 3 days.

SERVING SPREADS

Because spreads keep well, they can be made a day ahead and refrigerated until just before serving. If you do not plan to serve spreads on crackers or toast, offer them in small bowls or ramekins with the crackers alongside. Figure 1 to 2 tablespoons of spread per person.

Eggplant Caviar

8 to 10 appetizer servings

This dish from the Caucasus was originally created as a tasty substitute for those who could not afford the luxury of real caviar.

Preheat the oven to 375°F. Pierce in several places and roast on a baking sheet until soft, 45 to 60 minutes:

2 pounds eggplant (about 2 large)

Let stand until cool enough to handle. Peel the eggplants and finely chop. Heat in a large skillet over medium heat:

6 tablespoons olive oil

Add and cook, stirring occasionally, until soft, about 7 minutes:

2 medium onions, finely chopped
1 green bell pepper, finely chopped
2 tablespoons minced garlic

Add the eggplant along with:

One 28-ounce can plum tomatoes, drained and finely chopped
2 teaspoons salt
Ground black pepper to taste

Bring the mixture to a boil, reduce the heat to low, and simmer, covered, for 1 hour. Remove the cover and continue to simmer, stirring frequently, until the excess liquid has evaporated; the mixture should be thick but not dry. Stir in:

2 tablespoons fresh lemon juice

Taste and adjust the seasonings. Let cool, then cover and refrigerate for several hours before serving on:

Black or rye bread

Salmon Mousse

About 3 cups

Instead of molding (opposite), this easy mousse can also be decoratively piped through a pastry bag fitted with a large fluted tip onto or into sliced bread, cucumber cups, or cucumber slices.

Stir together in a saucepan or microwave-safe cup:

¼ cup fresh lemon juice
2¼ teaspoons (1 envelope) unflavored gelatin

Let stand for 5 minutes to soften. Heat for 1 to 2 minutes over medium heat or in a microwave, covered, on high until dissolved, about 40 seconds. Let cool for a few minutes, then stir in:

¼ cup mayonnaise
¼ cup sour cream

Combine in a food processor:

One 15-ounce can red salmon, drained, skin and bones removed
¼ cup chopped fresh dill
1 shallot, minced

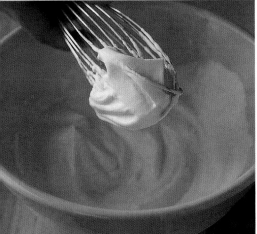

1 tablespoon drained capers, chopped cornichons, or pickle relish
1 teaspoon sweet paprika
Ground red or white pepper to taste

Pulse briefly just until combined. Do not overprocess. Add the gelatin mixture and pulse once just to combine. Beat until stiff peaks form:

¾ cup heavy cream

Gently fold the salmon mixture into the cream. Oil a decorative fish mold or a stainless-steel bowl. Transfer the salmon mixture to the oiled container, smooth the top, cover, and refrigerate until firm, 2 to 3 hours. To unmold, submerge two-thirds of the mold in very hot water for 20 to 30 seconds and immediately invert the mousse onto a serving platter. Garnish with:

Watercress sprigs, thinly sliced cucumber, or lemon wedges

Taramasalata (Pureed Fish Roe)

About ½ cup

This rich, creamy mixture is usually served as a spread with bread or crackers. True taram, *the salted and dried roe of gray mullet, is difficult to find. Smoked cod or carp roe is a good substitute and easier to find; rinse under cold running water to remove excess salt.*

Combine in a food processor or blender:

4 ounces smoked cod or carp roe or dried gray mullet roe
Juice of 1 large lemon

Add:

2 slices firm white bread, trimmed, soaked briefly in water, and squeezed dry

With the machine running, gradually pour in:

½ to ⅔ cup olive oil

Taste and add more lemon juice if desired. Transfer to a small bowl and stir in:

½ small onion, grated and squeezed dry with a paper towel

Refrigerate and serve chilled.

White Bean and Roasted Garlic Puree

About 2½ cups

This simple bean puree employs common pantry ingredients, which, when put together, result in a memorable spread for grilled or toasted French bread. Other fresh green herbs, such as parsley, thyme, or marjoram, can be substituted for the basil but should be added to taste.

Pick over, rinse, and soak in water to cover 8 to 12 hours:

1 cup dried cannellini, white kidney, great Northern, baby lima, or other white beans

Drain. Place in a large saucepan with enough water to cover by 2 inches and add:

1 bay leaf
1 sprig fresh thyme
1 thick onion wedge

Bring to a boil. Reduce the heat to low and cook, covered, until the beans are tender, about 1 hour. Drain, reserving ½ cup of the cooking liquid. Discard the bay leaf and thyme.

Meanwhile, preheat the oven to 325°F.

Combine in an 8-ounce custard cup or small baking dish:

6 large cloves garlic, crushed
2 tablespoons olive oil, preferably extra virgin

Cover with aluminum foil and bake until golden but not browned, about 35 minutes. Let cool slightly. In a food processor, puree the reserved cooking liquid with:

1 cup ½-inch cubes peeled baked potatoes
½ cup packed fresh basil leaves
1 teaspoon salt

Add the cooked beans and roasted garlic with oil. Process until smooth. Stir in:

⅛ teaspoon ground black pepper

Serve hot with:

Grilled or toasted French bread

Whipped Feta with Roasted Peppers

About 2 cups

This dip is a specialty of Macedonia. Its good flavor depends on the quality of the feta. Seek out an imported or good-quality domestic sheep's- or goat's-milk feta for the best results.

Combine in a food processor:

1 pound Greek feta cheese, crumbled
2 tablespoons extra-virgin olive oil

Pulse until the feta is creamy. Add:

1 red bell pepper, roasted, 18, peeled, seeded, and coarsely chopped
2 or 3 fresh jalapeño peppers, seeded and minced
2 pickled pepperoncini, rinsed, seeded, and minced
Several grindings of black pepper

Pulse until the mixture is well combined while gradually adding:

3 tablespoons extra-virgin olive oil
2 tablespoons fresh lemon juice

The feta should be creamy and spreadable. Taste and add more olive oil and/or lemon juice if desired. Serve with:

Crackers or pita bread

Blue Cheese Spread with Walnuts

About 1¼ cups

If serving with fruit slices, soak the fruit in a bowl of water mixed with a squeeze of lemon juice to prevent browning.

Puree in a food processor until smooth:

8 ounces cream cheese, softened
2 ounces blue cheese
2 tablespoons port (optional)

Scrape into a small bowl. Sprinkle with:

1 tablespoon chopped walnuts, toasted

Serve with:

Sliced French bread
Sliced apples and/or pears
Quartered fresh figs

TOASTING NUTS

To toast nuts in the oven, spread them on an ungreased baking sheet and bake in a 325°F oven for 5 to 7 minutes. Check and stir often to prevent burning.

Liptauer Cheese

About 1 cup

This is Hungary's famous spiced cheese spread (above).

Stir together until thoroughly blended:

8 ounces cream cheese, softened
2 teaspoons sweet Hungarian paprika

Stir in:

2 tablespoons finely minced onions
2 teaspoons drained capers, chopped
¾ teaspoon caraway seeds

Scrape into a small bowl and serve with:

Thinly sliced black or rye bread
Radishes (optional)

Cream-Cheese Chutney Spread

About 1½ cups

This old-fashioned spread is especially good with whole-wheat crackers.

Pulse in a food processor until combined:

8 ounces cream cheese, softened
6 tablespoons mango chutney

Scrape into a small bowl. Sprinkle with:

1 tablespoon chopped walnuts, toasted

Serve with:

Crackers

TURNING A SPREAD INTO A DIP

Most spreads can be turned into dips by thinning slightly with cream, lemon juice, vinegar, or mayonnaise.

ABOUT **CHEESE** PARTY FOODS

*I*n addition to the simple cheese-based delights in this chapter, consider serving a cheese platter as party food. Choose at least three varieties, each of a different type: for instance, one fresh goat cheese; one soft fermented cheese (such as Brie, Camembert, Pont-l'Évêque—the rind, incidentally, is edible); one blue-veined cheese (the classics are Roquefort from France, Gorgonzola from Italy, and Stilton from England, but there are many others, including a few splendid American examples); and one firm cheese (such as farmhouse Cheddar, caerphilly, good-quality provolone, Gruyère, Gouda, Manchego). Alternatively, a single perfect cheese may be served: irregular chunks of Parmigiano-Reggiano, for example, or a ripe whole Brie, or a cylinder of Stilton soft enough to be scooped out with a spoon.

Arrange the cheeses on a large board or tray with or without fruit. Present them whole to be sliced (or scooped up) as desired by the guests. Offer a variety of sliced breads, biscuits, and crackers on the side.

Clockwise from top left: New York Cheddar, Camembert, Vermont White Cheddar, Stilton, Parmigiano-Reggiano, chèvre (center)

Marinated Goat Cheese with Fresh Thyme

8 to 10 appetizer servings

Goat cheese logs are produced in a variety of sizes from small 4-ounce logs to huskier 10- or 11-ounce logs. This recipe is easily adapted to smaller or larger logs. Use two smaller logs or increase the ingredients by half and set out a larger 10-ounce log. Goat cheese marinated in olive oil with herbs is a staple of the Mediterranean larder.

Place in a shallow bowl:

One 7-ounce log goat cheese
2 tablespoons extra-virgin olive oil
1½ teaspoons fresh thyme leaves

Turn the cheese to coat. Marinate in the refrigerator, turning once or twice, for at least 1 hour or up to 5 days. Let warm to room temperature before serving, about 30 minutes. Serve with:

Sliced French bread, toasted

Goat Cheese with Cracked Pepper

8 to 10 appetizer servings

For a simple appetizer, serve with an assortment of olives and roasted pepper strips. Marinated goat cheese is also a welcome accompaniment to a platter of bruschetta and crostini, 20–21.

Crack with a mortar and pestle:

½ teaspoon whole black peppercorns

Roll in the peppercorns:

One 7-ounce log goat cheese

Set the cheese on a plate and drizzle over the top:

2 tablespoons extra-virgin olive oil

If desired, sprinkle with:

6 sun-dried tomato halves in oil, drained and chopped

Serve at room temperature with:

Sliced French bread, toasted

Bocconcini (Marinated Mozzarella)

6 to 8 appetizer servings

Warm in a medium skillet over medium heat:

1 cup olive oil

Add:

2 cloves garlic, thinly sliced
12 black peppercorns
3 large sprigs fresh rosemary
¼ teaspoon salt
Pinch of red pepper flakes

Remove from the heat and let cool to room temperature. Remove the rosemary sprigs. Pour the oil mixture over:

12 ounces fresh mozzarella, cut into 1-inch cubes

Let stand at room temperature for several hours or cover and refrigerate for up to 4 days. If refrigerated, bring to room temperature before serving.

SERVING CHEESE

There is a perfect point of ripeness (or rather there are several perfect points, depending on individual taste) for every cheese, and the storage of cheese until it reaches its optimum condition is a complicated art. Unless you train yourself to become a specialist, we recommend finding a good cheese merchant and, for company at least, buying cheeses that are ready to eat. Unless you're going to serve it the day you buy it, cheese should be stored, loosely wrapped, in the refrigerator. Cheese should always be removed from cold storage at least 3 hours before being served.

Cheese Fondue

2 to 3 cups; 4 to 6 servings

Legend has it that fondue was invented during a sixteenth-century siege of Zurich, when inhabitants had to feed themselves on a small stock of available ingredients—which fortunately included bread, cheese, and wine. The dish later became a tradition throughout German-speaking Switzerland and in the mountainous French region of Savoie. It was popular party fare in the United States in the 1950s and 1960s, and after a period in culinary disrepute is now enjoying a revival here.

Tear into bite-sized pieces:

1 loaf white country bread

Rub the interior of a medium stainless-steel pot with:

1 clove garlic, peeled and halved

Discard the garlic and add to the pot:

1¼ cups Swiss fendant or other dry white wine

Bring to a simmer over medium heat. Add:

1 pound Gruyère cheese, chopped
Pinch of freshly grated or ground nutmeg

Cook, stirring with a wooden spoon, until the cheese is melted (the cheese and wine will not yet be blended). Mix together thoroughly in a small bowl:

1 tablespoon cornstarch
2 tablespoons kirsch

Stir into the cheese mixture. Continue to stir and simmer until the cheese mixture is smooth, about 5 minutes. Season with:

Salt and ground black pepper

If the fondue is too thick, add up to:

¼ cup Swiss fendant or other dry white wine

To serve, transfer to a fondue pot or chafing dish set over a flame. To eat, spear bread pieces with fondue forks and dip in the cheese, continuing to stir the mixture with the forks as you dip.

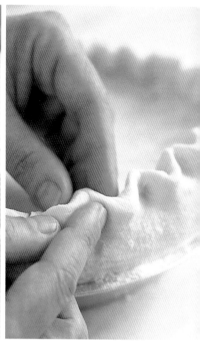

Brie Baked in Pastry

28 servings

Let warm to room temperature, 30 minutes to 1 hour:

One 17½-ounce package frozen puff pastry sheets

Unfold the two 9-inch squares and, on a lightly floured surface, gently roll out each into a 12-inch square. Center 1 sheet in a 9-inch pie pan. Top with:

One 1-kilogram Brie wheel (2.2 pounds, 8 inches in diameter)

If desired, spread the top of the cheese with:

3 to 4 tablespoons sweet chutney, finely chopped, or sweet preserves

Fold the pastry up and over the Brie, pleating the excess and trimming it to 1 inch over the top rim of the cheese. Cut the second pastry sheet into a circle the diameter of the Brie, using the top of the cheese box as a template. Lay the pastry circle on top of the Brie, gently roll the top and bottom edges together, and crimp to seal. Refrigerate for at least 30 minutes or up 24 hours. Preheat the oven to 400°F. Stir together in a small bowl:

1 large egg yolk
1 tablespoon milk

Using a pastry brush, gently brush the egg wash over the pastry. Bake for 10 minutes. Reduce the oven temperature to 350°F and bake until golden and puffy, 30 to 40 minutes. Let stand for 1 hour before serving. Serve in the pie pan or gently remove to a plate. Cut a small wedge and partially remove. Set out the Brie with a knife, surrounded by:

Sliced fresh or dried fruit
Sliced French bread

DRIED FRUITS

When selecting dried fruits, look for the biggest and brightest, the plumpest, and those with uniform color. Avoid fruits with blemishes and packages containing bits and pieces of stalks or damaged fruits. Check for unnecessary additives. When a new box or package is opened, do not store the fruits in the opened container. Dried fruits should be stored in tightly covered glass containers in a cool (45° to 50°F), dark, dry place or the refrigerator. Glass is good because you can see if any moisture is collecting inside—moisture will cause dry foods to spoil. Store dried fruits far from pungent foods like onions and garlic, because the fruits readily absorb other odors.

Herbed Laban (Yogurt Cheese)

About 20 balls

These tangy rounds are often served for breakfast in the Middle East, but they make an excellent appetizer when served on a platter with ripe tomatoes, marinated olives, and cucumber spears and accompanied with wedges of pita bread.

Mix well:

2 cups low-fat yogurt

2 teaspoons salt

Scrape into a colander lined with a triple layer of cheesecloth and let drain at room temperature for 24 hours. Turn out onto several layers of paper towels on a plate and refrigerate until almost dry to the touch, 6 to 10 hours. Mix together:

1 tablespoon sweet paprika

2 tablespoons minced fresh mint, or 1 tablespoon dried crumbled

Form the yogurt cheese into balls slightly larger than golf balls. Roll the balls in the mint mixture. Serve at once, or place in a jar and cover with:

Olive oil

Refrigerate until ready to use.

Savory Pesto Cheesecake

20 servings

Prepare:

Pesto Sauce, right

Preheat the oven to 375°F. Lightly butter an 8-inch springform pan. Dust the bottom and sides of the pan with:

Seasoned dry breadcrumbs

Mix together in a large bowl ½ cup of the pesto along with:

1 pound ricotta cheese

½ cup sour cream

4 large eggs

1 teaspoon salt

½ teaspoon grated lemon zest

½ teaspoon freshly grated or ground nutmeg

½ teaspoon ground black pepper

Pour into the prepared pan. Bake in a water bath, below, until set, 30 to 35 minutes. Remove from the water bath and transfer the pan to a rack to cool completely. Cover and refrigerate until cold, 6 to 12 hours. Slide a thin-bladed knife around the outside of the cake and remove the outer ring. Spread the remaining pesto around the sides of the cheesecake. Spread the top with an even layer of:

½ cup sour cream

If desired, arrange on the top:

12 sun-dried tomato halves in oil, drained and chopped

Serve cold or at room temperature with:

Sliced French bread, toasted

Pesto Sauce

About 1 cup

Process to a rough paste in a food processor:

2 cups loosely packed fresh basil leaves

⅓ cup pine nuts

2 medium cloves garlic, peeled

½ cup grated Parmesan cheese

With the machine running, slowly pour through the feed tube:

½ cup extra-virgin olive oil

If the sauce seems dry, add a little more olive oil. Season to taste with:

Salt and ground black pepper

HOW TO BAKE IN A WATER BATH

Wrap the bottom and sides of the springform pan to prevent water from seeping into the seams.

1 Set the pan on a wide sheet of heavy-duty aluminum foil. Fold the foil up the sides of the pan, making sure there are no rips or holes. For the water bath, choose a baking dish or roasting pan that is at least 3 inches wider, but that is no deeper, than the springform pan. Put a kettle of water on to boil when you preheat the oven. After filling the springform pan, set it in the baking dish. Slide the oven rack partway out and set the baking dish on it.

2 Carefully pour boiling water around the springform pan to a depth of about 1 inch. Slide the oven rack back gently to avoid sloshing.

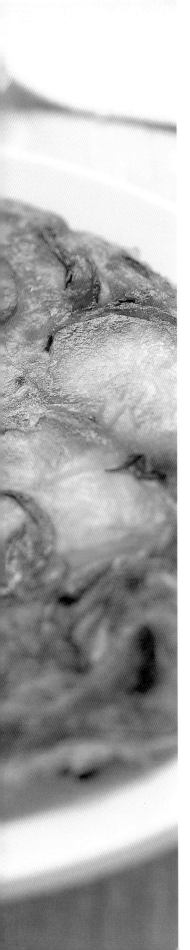

ABOUT
FRUIT &
VEGETABLE
PARTY FOODS

*T*he produce department, greengrocer, farmers' market, or home garden yield a cornucopia of easy options for party foods. Many fruits and vegetables require little more than rinsing and trimming or cutting up to make them ready for serving.

Fruit offers a light, refreshing counterpoint to the more common savory party foods. During the summer months, when a great variety of fruit is available, a large fruit platter can be a magnificent centerpiece on a buffet table.

Cooked or raw vegetables make some of the most colorful and appreciated party foods. They range from the assorted raw vegetable platter known as Crudités, 50, *to popular cooked vegetables such as potatoes and mushrooms.*

When serving fruits or vegetables as party foods, let seasonality guide your decisions. Look for whatever is freshest in the market or garden before you choose the recipes you'll prepare.

Tortilla Española, 54

Serving Fruit for a Party

Keep the pieces large and arrange them according to size, color, and shape rather than tossing them together like a salad. Mix styles on the same platter by combining cut melons, pineapple, or other fruit with some whole fruit with stems, like berries, small clusters of seedless grapes, or cherries on the stem. Use fruit leaves for garnish if available. For a spicy arrangement, make a platter of sliced peeled honeydew melon, watermelon, cantaloupe, mango, green apple, and jícama (though a vegetable, it is a lovely addition to a fruit platter) and just before serving, sprinkle the platter with lime juice or a mixture of salt and chili powder. Also consider skewered fruits served with a sweetened dip—for instance, a mixture of vanilla yogurt, honey, mint, and lemon zest. Grilled fruits such as pineapple, plums, peaches, and bananas, served on or with skewers or toothpicks, are another possibility. Single fruit trays are also dramatic. Try serving a large basket of strawberries with a bowl of sour cream and another of brown sugar, or melon balls or strawberries wrapped in prosciutto. In the winter months, try a platter of red-skinned pear wedges served with a soft blue cheese for spreading.

Melon and Figs Wrapped in Prosciutto

6 appetizer servings

Prosciutto means "ham" in Italian, and it is exquisite ham. Prosciutto needs no cooking and, in fact, can become dry and tough if cooked. Instead, it is commonly served sliced paper-thin with sliced melons or figs. Look for prosciutto di Parma imported from Italy and avoid domestic varieties of unsmoked, salt-cured ham, which do not compare.
Seed, thinly slice, and remove the rind from:

1 small honeydew melon or large cantaloupe
Halve through the stem end:

6 fresh figs
Wrap each melon slice and fig half separately in:

1 paper-thin slice prosciutto (about 8 ounces total)
Serve at room temperature (opposite).

SLICING MELON
Slice the melon in half through the stem end and scoop out the seeds and loose pulp or strings. Slice each half into 2-inch-thick wedges and cut off the rind at the point where it changes to the color of the flesh. Continue slicing peeled pieces into thin crescents.

Grilled Peaches with Sweet Balsamic Glaze

4 servings

To prevent the peaches from sticking to the grill, oil them very lightly before cooking, but use a light hand. Too much oil not only will interfere with the taste of the fruit but also can cause flare-ups if it drips into the fire.
Combine in a small wide-mouthed saucepan:

1 cup balsamic vinegar
2 tablespoons sugar
1 teaspoon cracked black peppercorns
Bring to a boil, reduce the heat to low, and simmer, stirring occasionally, for 30 to 45 minutes or until reduced in volume by about two-thirds and thick enough to coat the back of a spoon. Set aside.
Prepare a medium-hot charcoal fire. Lightly brush:

3 firm, ripe peaches, halved and pitted
with:

1 tablespoon olive oil
Grill the peaches, skin side down, until slightly charred, about 4 to 5 minutes per side. Brush with the glaze and grill until the glaze begins to caramelize slightly, about 1 minute. Remove the peaches from the grill, brush on another layer of glaze, slice into thick slices, and serve, accompanied with:

⅓ cup crumbled blue cheese (optional)

Vegetables for Crudités

The best vegetables for any selection of crudités are those that are freshest in the market (or your garden) on the day you are making it. For maximum visual effect, arrange the vegetables in a large basket or on a platter, interspersing those with brighter colors (radishes, bell peppers, carrots) among those of a more subdued hue (scallions, celery, cauliflower, mushrooms). For a casual affair, a single dip or salad dressing for drizzling over the vegetables is sufficient. If the crudités are the centerpiece of a buffet of little dishes, you might want to offer several dipping options.

Crudités

6 to 8 appetizer servings

Crudités *refers to an assortment of raw vegetables. In France, this usually means a kind of untossed salad, for instance, quartered tomatoes and shredded carrots, both moistened with vinaigrette, celery root dressed with sauce rémoulade, and some neatly trimmed radishes. In the United States, the term has come to mean an assortment of raw vegetables, often cut into chunks or strips, with a dip on the side.* Decoratively arrange in a large basket or on a platter:

About 6 cups assorted vegetables, rinsed, seeded, and trimmed as needed, such as:
Cauliflower florets
Radishes
Carrot sticks
Celery sticks
Cucumber spears
Zucchini strips
Mushrooms
Snow peas
Bell peppers, cut into eighths
Fennel strips
Green beans, blanched
Romaine lettuce hearts
Scallions
Cherry tomatoes
Cooked beets, cut into strips
Garnish as desired with:
Green and/or black olives
Large fresh parsley and/or rosemary sprigs
Set out one or more of the following for dipping and drizzling over the top:
Any salad dressing
Any dip, 24 to 30
Garlic Mayonnaise, right
Tapenade, 32

Garlic Mayonnaise

Whisk together in a medium bowl until smooth and light:
2 large egg yolks
4 to 6 cloves garlic, finely minced
Salt and ground white pepper to taste
Whisk in by drops until the mixture starts to thicken and stiffen:
1 cup olive oil
As the sauce begins to thicken, whisk in the oil more steadily. Gradually whisk in:
1 teaspoon fresh lemon juice, or to taste
½ teaspoon cold water
Taste and adjust the seasonings. Serve immediately or refrigerate for 1 to 2 days.

Fennel Wrapped in Prosciutto

12 appetizer servings

A bulb of fennel looks like a bunch of celery with a wide, round base. The individual stalks, which are beautifully plaited, are broad and thin, while the tops are round and fleshy. Fennel leaves are ferny, and the flavor of the whole plant is like licorice.

Trim the top and ¼ inch from the bottom of:

1 fennel bulb (about 1 pound)

Cut in half vertically, then cut crosswise into about thirty-six ¼-inch slices. Wrap each fennel piece in:

1 paper-thin slice prosciutto (about 4 ounces total)

Arrange on a serving platter and sprinkle with:

2 ounces Parmesan cheese, thinly shaved

Sprinkle over the top:

1 tablespoon extra-virgin olive oil

Ground black pepper to taste

Serve at room temperature.

Stuffed Celery

24 pieces

Use a spoon, pastry bag, or plastic bag with a cut corner to stuff the celery. Fill the hollows of:

Twenty-four 3-inch-long pieces celery, leaves intact if possible

with 1¼ to 1½ cups of any of the following:

Cream cheese, softened

Salmon Mousse, 34

Blue Cheese Spread with Walnuts, 36

Garnish with:

Chopped walnuts or fresh parsley

Marinated Olives with Lemon, Thyme, and Rosemary

About 4 cups

Combine well:

4 cups mixed green and black brine-cured olives

1 tablespoon fresh thyme, or 2 teaspoons dried

6 sprigs fresh rosemary, or 2 tablespoons dried

Zest of about ½ lemon, thinly slivered

4 cloves garlic, very thinly slivered

¼ cup extra-virgin olive oil

2 tablespoons fresh lemon juice

Salt and freshly cracked black peppercorns to taste

Pinch of red pepper flakes

Cover and refrigerate for 1 to 2 days, stirring several times. Serve with:

Crusty French bread

The olives will keep, covered and refrigerated, for several weeks.

Mixed Marinated Olives, Spanish Style

About 4 cups

Combine in a small saucepan:

1 cup Spanish olive oil

2 sprigs fresh rosemary

3 cloves garlic, very finely minced

2 bay leaves

½ teaspoon coarsely ground black pepper

Pinch of red pepper flakes

Bring to a bare simmer over medium heat. Immediately remove from the heat, stir once or twice, and let cool to room temperature. Meanwhile, rinse with warm water, drain, and dry well with paper towels:

2 cups brine-cured green olives

1 cup oil-cured black olives

1 cup small brine-cured black olives

Place the olives in a glass or earthenware container and pour the oil over them. Let cool completely, then cover and keep in a cool place for up to 1 week. Bring to room temperature before serving.

MEDITERRANEAN OLIVES

In the Mediterranean region, where most olives are grown, as much care is put into olive growing as into wine or cheese making; to classify olives as being simply green or black would not do justice to the wealth of piquant, nutty, sweet, and fruity olives available. If an olive is green, it has been harvested when it has grown to normal size but just before it has ripened. A black olive is allowed to fully ripen to a rich dark-purple hue before harvesting. Otherwise, the differences between types of olives are in how they are cured and processed.

Potato Patties

About twenty-four 1½-inch patties

Drop into boiling water to cover:

1½ pounds boiling potatoes (6 to 8 potatoes)

Cover and cook until tender, 25 to 30 minutes. Drain, remove the skins, and mash. Heat in a medium skillet over high heat:

1 tablespoon canola or other vegetable oil

Add and stir-fry until they pop:

1 teaspoon black or yellow mustard seeds

Add and stir-fry for 20 seconds more:

3 cloves garlic, thinly sliced

Stir the garlic mixture into the mashed potatoes along with:

1 small onion, chopped (about ½ cup)

¼ cup chopped fresh cilantro

1 serrano or jalapeño pepper, seeded, if desired, and minced

2 tablespoons fresh lemon juice

1¼ teaspoons salt

Shape the mixture into 1½-inch patties and cook in batches, without crowding, in a lightly oiled skillet until lightly browned on both sides, 1 to 2 minutes each side. Serve at once, accompanied with:

Fresh Mint-Cilantro Chutney, right

Fresh Mint-Cilantro Chutney

About 1 cup

Combine in a food processor or blender and puree:

1 cup lightly packed fresh mint leaves

½ cup lightly packed fresh cilantro leaves

½ cup coarsely chopped onions

3 small scallions, chopped

3 fresh jalapeño peppers, seeded and chopped

3 tablespoons water

1½ tablespoons fresh lemon juice

¼ teaspoon salt

Cover and refrigerate.

Crispy Potato Skins

16 skins; 4 servings

To make the garlic butter, in a small bowl, cream with a fork:

4 tablespoons (½ stick) butter, softened

Add:

1 to 3 cloves garlic, boiled in water to cover for 5 to 6 minutes, mashed to a paste

Set aside. Scoop out the flesh from:

4 baking potatoes, baked and quartered lengthwise

Preheat the oven to 500°F.

Melt in a large skillet over medium-high heat:

2 tablespoons butter

Add half the potato skins and cook, stirring, until golden brown. Remove to paper towels to drain. Spread the insides with the garlic butter. Place on a baking sheet and crisp in the oven for about 5 minutes. Repeat with the remaining potato skins.

New Potatoes Stuffed with Bacon and Cheese

24 little potatoes

Preheat the oven to 425°F.

Whisk together in a medium bowl:

2 tablespoons butter, melted (optional)

1 teaspoon Dijon mustard

Halve:

Twelve 1½- to 2-inch new potatoes

With the large end of a melon baller, hollow out each half, leaving ¼-inch shells. Immediately toss the halves in the mustard mixture. Roast, cut side down, on a lightly oiled baking sheet until nicely browned, 20 to 30 minutes. Sprinkle with:

Coarse salt

Turn the potatoes upright and divide equally among the skins:

¾ cup grated pepper Jack cheese

Sprinkle equally with:

8 slices bacon, cooked until crisp and crumbled

Return the potatoes to the oven and bake until hot, about 5 minutes. If desired, garnish with:

Sour cream

Sliced scallion greens

New Potatoes Stuffed with Sour Cream and Caviar

24 little potatoes

Prepare the potatoes as directed for *New Potatoes Stuffed with Bacon and Cheese,* left, omitting the mustard or, if desired, omitting both the butter and the mustard and roasting them cut side up. If you would rather not

scoop the potatoes out, slice them instead and top with the sour cream and caviar. Let the potatoes cool for 5 minutes, then sprinkle with:

Coarse salt

Spoon or pipe into each potato skin

or onto each potato slice:

1 teaspoon sour cream

Top each potato with:

⅛ to ½ teaspoon caviar or other roe

Sprinkle generously with:

Snipped fresh chives

Tortilla Española (Potato Omelet)

12 wedges

In the United States, when we make a Spanish omelet, it is a rolled one filled with peppers and tomatoes—but this authentic Spanish version is flat (but usually thick) and filled with potatoes and onions. Tortilla means "little cake" and in this case has nothing to do with the "little cakes" of corn or wheat flour called tortillas in Mexico and Central America. In flat omelets, eggs assume a supporting role, binding the savory ingredients and adding richness while the emphasis is on the filling. A flat omelet can be thick or thin, but it is always too hearty and awkward to roll or fold; instead, it is served in wedges, much like an open-faced pizza. Flat omelets can be made ahead and served at room temperature.

Heat in a large skillet over medium heat:

2 tablespoons olive oil

Add:

1 large onion (about 8 ounces), cut into ⅛-inch-thick slices
Salt and ground black pepper to taste

Cook until the onions are soft and golden, reducing the heat as they cook, about 20 minutes. Remove to a large bowl. Heat in the same skillet over high heat:

¼ cup olive oil

Add:

1 pound red-skinned potatoes, peeled and cut into ⅛-inch-thick slices

Cook until golden brown, 10 to 12 minutes. Reduce the heat to medium-high if the oil gets too hot and smoky. Toss the potatoes often with a metal spatula, separating the slices that stick together. Some will stick together no matter what you do, and that is fine. Remove the potatoes with a slotted spoon to paper towels to drain. Set aside the pan with the oil in it. Add to the onions and mix together:

6 large eggs, lightly beaten
½ teaspoon salt
Ground black pepper to taste

Sprinkle the potatoes with:

Salt and ground black pepper to taste

Add the potatoes to the egg mixture and toss to coat the slices well with the egg. Return the skillet to high heat to heat the remaining oil in the pan. When hot, add the egg mixture and immediately reduce the heat to low. Let the omelet cook for 3 to 4 minutes, undisturbed, until the bottom is golden and the egg is two-thirds to three-quarters set. Shake the pan from time to time to make sure the omelet does not stick. If it does, slide a metal spatula under the egg to free it from the pan and continue cooking. Place a lightly oiled large heatproof plate upside down over the omelet and flip the skillet to turn the omelet over. Slide the omelet back into the pan to cook the second side. Cook until golden and set, 2 to 3 minutes more. Shake the omelet loose from the pan and slide onto a clean plate. Cut into 12 thin wedges and serve hot or at room temperature.

STORING POTATOES

Potatoes should be stored unwashed and unwrapped. Be sure to keep them in a cool, dark, dry, and well-ventilated place.

Mushrooms Stuffed with Breadcrumbs and Herbs

24 mushrooms

These stuffed mushrooms (or the variation that follows) may be frozen unbaked for up to 2 weeks, but for best results, cook them fresh. If frozen, thaw for 1 hour, then bake as directed.
Preheat the oven to 375°F.
Remove and reserve the stems from:

20 ounces mushrooms, wiped clean
Count out 24 same-sized mushroom caps and toss with:

1 to 2 tablespoons butter, melted, or olive oil
Slice the remaining caps. Rinse and chop the stems. Heat in a medium skillet:

2 tablespoons butter or olive oil
Add the sliced and chopped mushrooms along with:

1 large shallot, minced

½ teaspoon dried thyme
Cook, stirring occasionally, over medium heat for 5 minutes. Stir in:

¾ cup dry or fresh unseasoned breadcrumbs

3 tablespoons snipped fresh chives or chopped fresh basil or tarragon

2 tablespoons dry vermouth or sherry
Transfer to a food processor and coarsely chop. Season with:

Salt and ground black pepper to taste
Fill each mushroom cap with 1 heaping teaspoon of the filling. Place on a baking sheet. Sprinkle with:

2 to 3 tablespoons grated Parmesan cheese
Bake until the tops are bubbling, about 15 minutes. Serve warm.

CLEANING MUSHROOMS

Clean mushrooms with a soft brush (**1**) or wipe with a damp cloth (**2**). Or if the mushrooms are truly grimy, rinse them quickly under cold running water and pat dry. Never soak mushrooms—their delicate tissues will absorb water. If desired, slice ⅛ inch off the bottom of the stems to refresh them but do not discard the flavorful stems.

Mushrooms Stuffed with Sausage

24 mushrooms

Heat a medium skillet over medium heat. Add:

12 ounces sweet or hot sausage links, casings removed, or bulk sausage

2 teaspoons minced garlic
Cook for 5 minutes, stirring to break up the meat. Stir in:

½ cup dry or fresh unseasoned breadcrumbs

¼ cup chopped roasted red peppers or pimientos

3 tablespoons minced fresh parsley
Prepare *Mushrooms Stuffed with Breadcrumbs and Herbs, above,* discarding the mushroom stems and substituting the sausage mixture for the mushroom filling. Sprinkle with the cheese and bake as directed.

SELECTING MUSHROOMS

Choose mushrooms that are heavy for their size, with dry, firm caps and stems—nothing damp or shriveled, no dark or soft spots, and all close to the same size. If gills are open, the mushrooms are more mature and their flavor will be stronger, and with a wild mushroom, this may be a plus. Open-gilled mushrooms should be used as soon as possible.

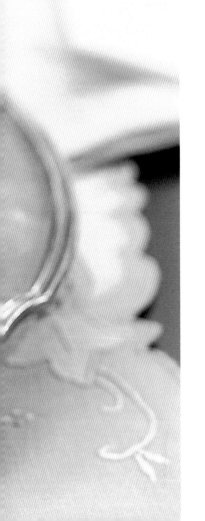

ABOUT **PASTRY** PARTY FOODS

*B*ecause it keeps so well in the freezer, pastry is a perfect choice for elegant party foods that can be at least partially prepared in advance. Pastry dough, for instance, can be rolled, cut, shaped, and frozen, then removed from the freezer at the proper time, filled, and baked. Phyllo (also called filo) pastries, such as those on pages 62 to 65, can be completely assembled and then frozen, later to be baked straight from the freezer.

Gougères, 59, with (center) Parmesan Straws, 60

Choux Paste

About 2½ cups

Choux paste can be frozen in its uncooked state and removed the day before the party to thaw overnight in the refrigerator. The morning of the party, pipe the dough into shapes and bake the puffs.

Measure:

1 cup sifted all-purpose flour

Combine in a large saucepan:

½ cup water

½ cup whole milk

8 tablespoons (1 stick) unsalted butter, cut into small pieces

½ teaspoon salt

Bring the mixture to a full boil over medium heat. Add the flour all at once and stir vigorously with a wooden spoon until the mixture pulls away from the sides of the pan.

Continue to cook and stir the mixture for about 1 minute, to eliminate excess moisture. The butter may ooze out, which is fine; it simply means that the moisture is evaporating. Transfer to a bowl and let cool for 5 minutes, stirring occasionally. Beat in 1 at a time by hand, with a wooden spoon, or on low speed with a mixer:

4 large eggs

Make sure that the paste is smooth before adding the next egg. Beat the dough until it is smooth and shiny. Choux paste can be covered and refrigerated for up to 4 hours. When it is cold, you do not need to bring the paste to room temperature before shaping.

HOW TO FORM SMALL CHOUX PUFFS

1 Fit a ½-inch plain pastry tip in the bottom of a pastry bag. Twist and stuff the bottom of the bag into the tip to prevent the choux paste from leaking out before you are ready to pipe. If you are right-handed, hold the bag in your left hand (if you are left-handed, use the opposite hand throughout). Fold the top 3 to 4 inches of the pastry bag down over your hand like a cuff. Scoop the choux paste into the bag, filling it no more than two-thirds full. (You can also place the bag in a 2-cup glass measure, leaving both hands free to fill the bag.) Unfold the cuff and squeeze the bag to push the choux paste toward the tip. Twist the top part of the bag. Unstuff the lower part of the bag from the tip and push the paste farther into the tip.

2 Hold the bag with the tip at a 90-degree angle to the baking sheet. On an ungreased baking sheet, pipe puffs 1 inch wide and 1 inch high.

3 To stop piping, release pressure from the bag before lifting the tip, then push the tip down and quickly jerk it upward to end the shape without a tail. Pipe shapes about 2 inches apart to allow for expansion.

4 After piping the shapes, smooth out the points with a finger dipped in cold water. As the bag is depleted, slide your hand forward, pressing the paste toward the tip. Or, spoon out shapes and smooth them with a finger dipped in cold water. Spoon out a scant tablespoon per puff.

Gougères
(Cheese Puffs)

About 48 small puffs

These Burgundian cheese puffs, as light as air when made properly, are an elegantly simple party food. Pass them on a pretty tray and serve with Champagne.

Position a rack in the lower third of the oven. Preheat the oven to 400°F.
Stir:

1 cup grated Gruyère cheese
into:

1 recipe Choux Paste, opposite
Pipe as directed for small puffs, opposite. Sprinkle with:

½ cup grated Gruyère cheese
Bake for 15 minutes. Reduce the oven temperature to 350°F and continue to bake until golden brown and very firm to the touch, 10 to 15 minutes more.
Serve warm.

Choux Puffs with Lobster Salad

About 24 small puffs

Lobster salad is elegant and subtle. It makes a splendid filling for choux puffs. Baked choux puffs can also be filled with egg salad, shrimp salad, or chicken salad. Creamy fillings like Chicken Liver Pâté, 88, *and* Salmon Mousse, 34, *can be piped into the unsplit puffs.*
Prepare:

½ recipe Choux Paste, opposite
Form into twenty-four 1-inch puffs on a baking sheet. Bake as directed for *Gougères, above,* and cool.
Combine in a medium bowl:

1 cup chopped or shredded cooked lobster meat

¼ cup sour cream, mayonnaise, or yogurt

⅓ cup thinly sliced seeded, peeled cucumber (optional)

½ hard-boiled egg, chopped (optional)
Stir in:

1½ tablespoons slivered blanched snow peas

1½ teaspoons finely snipped fresh chives

1½ teaspoons minced fresh parsley

½ teaspoon minced fresh tarragon leaves

½ teaspoon fresh lemon juice

Pinch of grated lemon zest
Split puffs and fill with lobster salad. Serve immediately.

DRYING CHOUX PUFFS

Choux paste is baked in a hot oven for the first few minutes to cause quick expansion; the temperature is then reduced to finish the baking and dry out the hollow shells. To further dry out the shells and allow more room for the filling, turn off the oven and let the puffs dry for about 10 minutes. For small puffs, pop them off the sheets, poke a small hole in the bottoms with a skewer or the tip of a small, sharp knife, and turn them upside down on the sheets for drying. For larger puffs, slide a spatula under the shapes to loosen them and poke them in a few places on the sides.

Food Processor Cheese Straws

About 32 straws

Preheat the oven to 350°F.

Place in a food processor:

8 tablespoons (1 stick) unsalted butter, softened

8 ounces sharp Cheddar or blue cheese, cut into chunks

Add:

1½ cups all-purpose flour

¼ teaspoon salt

¼ to ½ teaspoon ground red pepper

1 teaspoon Worcestershire sauce

Process until the mixture comes together; then press the dough together, wrap it in plastic, and chill for 30 minutes. Divide the dough into 4 equal pieces and roll each piece out between 2 sheets of wax paper to ⅛ inch thick. Cut into 6 x ½-inch strips. Twist, if desired, or form into other shapes. Arrange the pieces on 1 or 2 ungreased cookie sheets. Alternatively, use a cookie press outfitted with a houndstooth or star dispenser. Push the dough out onto an ungreased cookie sheet to make individual "straws." Bake until crisp and lightly browned, about 15 minutes. For a darker color, bake longer. Remove the sheet to a rack and let cool completely.

Parmesan Straws

About 32 straws

Cheese straws are a perfect way to use puff pastry scraps.

Roll out evenly into a 17 x 9-inch rectangle:

1 pound Food Processor Puff Pastry, opposite

Transfer the pastry to an ungreased baking sheet. Cover and refrigerate the dough for at least 30 minutes or wrap airtight and freeze until ready to use.

If the dough is frozen, let it thaw for a few minutes before cutting. Quickly transfer the pastry to a cutting board, trim ½ inch from all the sides to make a 16 x 8-inch rectangle, and cut into two 8-inch squares.

Lightly brush the squares with:

1 egg, lightly beaten

Sprinkle over 1 square:

½ cup grated dry cheese, such as Parmesan, pecorino, aged Asiago, or a combination

Salt and ground black pepper to taste

Roll lightly with the rolling pin to embed the cheese. Brush any cheese that clings to the rolling pin back onto the pastry. Place the second square, egg side down, on top of the cheese. Roll the cheese-filled dough into a 17 x 9-inch rectangle. Return to the baking sheet and refrigerate for 30 minutes.

Transfer the dough to a cutting board. Butter the baking sheet generously. Trim the pastry ½ inch all around, then cut the dough crosswise into 8 x ½-inch strips. Twist each strip by holding one end on the work surface and twisting the other end about 3 revolutions. Place the twisted strips at least 1 inch apart on the baking sheet, pressing the ends down firmly so that they don't untwist.

Refrigerate or freeze until firm while the oven preheats.

Position a rack in the lower third of the oven. Preheat the oven to 425°F. Bake the cheese straws until they are light brown, 12 to 15 minutes. Remove the sheet to a rack and let cool completely before serving.

Food Processor Puff Pastry

2¾ pounds

A modernized puff pastry recipe.
Pulse to combine in a food processor:

2⅓ cups all-purpose flour

1¼ teaspoons salt

Scatter over the flour:

5 tablespoons cold unsalted butter, cut into ½-inch cubes

Pulse until the mixture resembles coarse crumbs. Stir to combine:

½ cup ice water

2 tablespoons fresh lemon juice

1 large egg yolk

Drizzle the mixture over the contents of the processor. Pulse just until the dough begins to come together. Scrape the dough onto a sheet of plastic wrap and form it into a 5-inch square. Wrap the dough and refrigerate for 1 hour.

Cut into ½-inch slices and freeze for 2 minutes:

28 tablespoons (3½ sticks) unsalted butter

Place in a food processor:

1 cup all-purpose flour

Distribute the butter slices over the flour and pulse just until the mixture looks like fine gravel; it should not be processed to a paste. Scrape the

mixture onto a sheet of plastic wrap, cover, and shape into a 6-inch square. Wrap and refrigerate while rolling out the dough.

Remove the 5-inch dough square from the refrigerator. Place it on a lightly floured surface and roll into a 13 × 8-inch rectangle, keeping one 8-inch side facing you. Brush off the excess flour. Remove the butter patty from the refrigerator, unwrap it, and center it on one half of the dough (**1**). Fold the dough over the butter, completely covering it. Press the dough together on the 3 open sides. Turn the dough so that the folded edge is on the left, with one of the sealed sides (where the dough was pressed together) on the right to change the direction of the pastry for the next roll. The dough is now ready for turns.

Roll the dough package into a 17 × 7½-inch rectangle, keeping one short side of the rectangle facing you. Slide a metal dough scraper or spatula under the bottom third of the dough and fold it up. Slide the spatula under the top third of the dough and fold it down on top of the first third, as though you

were folding a business letter (**2**). This rolling and folding is called a single turn. Rotate the dough so that the folded edge is on the left and the open edge is on the right (like a book about to be opened). Roll the dough once more into a 17 × 7½-inch rectangle. This time fold the bottom end up and the top end down to meet in the center (rather than overlapping), then fold the dough in half so that the folded ends meet to make 4 layers of dough (**3**). This double fold is the second turn. Mark the dough with 2 imprints to remind yourself that you have given the dough 2 turns. Wrap the dough and refrigerate for 45 minutes. With the folded edge on the left and the open edge on the right, roll the dough out again to 17 × 7½ inches. Repeat the double fold for the third turn. Mark with 3 imprints, wrap the dough, and refrigerate for 45 minutes. Roll the dough out and repeat the double fold for the fourth turn. Mark the dough with 4 imprints, wrap, and refrigerate for at least 1 hour or up to 24 hours. The puff pastry is ready to use.

Working with Phyllo

Phyllo (also called filo) pastry dough leaves, basic to a number of cuisines all over the Middle East, eastern Europe, and Greece, can be found in the frozen food section of your supermarket. Thin and fragile, the pastry can be quite intimidating to the uninitiated, but it is easy to use if you follow these rules: Thaw the pastry in the refrigerator or at room temperature, remove it from the box, open the sheets out flat (they will be rolled in the package), and immediately cover the stack with a damp clean dish towel. Use one sheet at a time, keeping the rest covered. Brush each layer and the tops of the formed pastry with melted butter to keep it from drying and flaking. Don't worry about small tears.

PORCINI

Porcini, also called cèpes or boletes, look like very large button mushrooms with thick stalks and reddish caps. They are among the tastiest of wild mushrooms. Look for fresh porcini in late spring and fall. When fresh porcini are not available, look for dried (above). They need to be rinsed well and soaked before cooking. So flavorful are dried porcini mushrooms that the water in which they soak becomes well flavored, too. It needs to be strained before use.

Mushroom Triangles

About 36 triangles

If the edges of the phyllo dough are dry, you may end up with fewer triangles.

Combine in a small bowl:

½ ounce dried porcini or other dried mushrooms, such as shiitake

1 cup hot water or white wine

Let stand for 30 minutes. Strain the liquid through a fine-mesh sieve lined with a dampened paper towel, reserving the liquid, and finely chop the mushrooms. Melt in a medium skillet over medium heat:

2 tablespoons butter

Add and cook, stirring constantly, for 1 minute:

2 tablespoons minced shallots

1 teaspoon minced garlic

Add the chopped dried mushrooms along with:

6 ounces cremini, shiitake, or button mushrooms, wiped clean, stems trimmed, coarsely chopped

Cook, stirring occasionally, until the mushrooms begin to wilt, about 3 minutes. Add:

3 tablespoons reserved mushroom soaking liquid

2 tablespoons minced fresh parsley

½ teaspoon salt

¼ teaspoon ground black pepper, or to taste

Cook, stirring occasionally, until the mixture is almost dry, about 5 minutes. Transfer to a bowl and let cool completely. If desired, stir in:

2 ounces goat cheese

Preheat the oven to 375°F.

Melt in a small saucepan:

4 tablespoons (½ stick) butter

Cover with a damp dish towel on a work surface:

8 sheets frozen phyllo dough, thawed

Remove 1 sheet and brush it with melted butter. Lay another sheet over the first and cut lengthwise into 9 strips. Working with 1 strip at a time, spoon 1 teaspoon of the filling at the bottom left corner of the strip. Fold the bottom end over the filling to meet the right-hand edge, making a triangle; continue to fold, as if folding a flag, all the way to the top. Place on a baking sheet. Repeat with the remaining strips. Brush the tops with melted butter. Repeat with the remaining phyllo and filling. Bake until golden brown, about 15 minutes. Serve hot.

Spinach and Feta Triangles

About 36 triangles

This is a classic Greek combination.
Melt in a small skillet over medium heat:

2 tablespoons butter

Add and cook, stirring, for about 5 minutes:

¼ cup minced onions

Add:

One 10-ounce package frozen chopped spinach or mustard greens, thawed and well drained (about 1 cup)

Cook over medium heat until the juices are evaporated, about 5 minutes. Remove to a medium bowl and let cool. Stir in:

4 ounces feta cheese, crumbled
1 teaspoon fresh lemon juice
½ teaspoon ground black pepper

Proceed as for *Mushroom Triangles*, opposite, substituting the spinach mixture for the mushroom filling.

Samosas with Potatoes and Peas

About 60 samosas

Samosas, traditionally filled with a ground meat or a spicy potato mixture, like the one here, are usually eaten as a snack in India and make an excellent party food. Phyllo dough replaces the traditional pastry in which the filling is wrapped. These little pastries freeze very well when wrapped in plastic and can be baked frozen—simply add 5 minutes to the baking time.

Preheat the oven to 375°F. Butter 2 baking sheets.

Unroll on a dry work surface:

1 pound phyllo dough, thawed if frozen

Cover with a dry towel and cover the dry towel with a damp towel. Prepare the mixture for:

Potato Patties, 52

Fold into the potato mixture:

1 cup frozen peas, thawed

Melt:

8 tablespoons (1 stick) butter

Remove 1 sheet of the phyllo and lay it on the work surface, with a long side facing you. Brush lightly with melted butter, lay a second sheet on top, and brush it with melted butter. Cut the sheets vertically into 2½-inch-wide strips (the last strip will be only 2 inches). Cover the strips with a sheet of wax paper or plastic wrap and cover that with a damp towel. Working with 1 strip at a time, scoop up a rounded teaspoon of the potato mixture and pat it over the bottom right-hand corner of the strip, so that it fills the entire corner, not just the center. Fold the corner to the other side to make a triangle and continue folding to the end of the strip, as if folding a flag. Place on a baking sheet and brush the top with melted butter. Repeat with the remaining phyllo and filling. Bake until lightly browned, about 15 minutes. Serve immediately.

SAMOSAS WITH GROUND BEEF

Heat 2 tablespoons canola or other vegetable oil in a large skillet. Add and cook 1 medium onion, chopped (about 1 cup), stirring over medium heat until limp, about 3 minutes. Add ¾ teaspoon garlic paste (or 1 teaspoon minced garlic), ¾ teaspoon fresh ginger paste (or 1 teaspoon minced peeled fresh ginger), ¾ teaspoon ground coriander, ½ teaspoon turmeric, and ¾ teaspoon salt. Cook, stirring, for 2 minutes. Add 1 pound lean ground beef. Cook, stirring, until the meat is cooked through, about 5 minutes. Add ½ cup water. Simmer until the water has evaporated, 3 to 4 minutes. Stir in ¼ cup chopped fresh cilantro and 2 serrano or jalapeño peppers, seeded and minced. Fill and bake the samosas as directed for *Samosas with Potatoes and Peas, left.*

Small Olive Pastries

About 36 pastries

Heat in a large, heavy skillet over medium heat:

3 tablespoons extra-virgin olive oil

Add and cook, stirring often, until wilted, 5 to 7 minutes:

1 small fennel bulb, trimmed and coarsely chopped (about ⅔ cup)

1 cup coarsely chopped red onions

Remove to a medium bowl and add:

2 cups pitted Kalamata olives, rinsed and coarsely chopped

2 teaspoons chopped fresh oregano

½ teaspoon ground fennel seeds or 2 tablespoons ouzo

Toss well to combine and let stand at room temperature for 20 minutes. Meanwhile, preheat the oven to 375°F. Lightly oil 2 baking sheets. Unroll onto a dry work surface:

1 pound phyllo dough, thawed if frozen

Cover with a dry towel and cover the dry towel with a damp towel. Removing 1 sheet of phyllo at a time, place the phyllo in front of you, cut it lengthwise in half, and brush each half lightly with:

Extra-virgin olive oil

Fold each strip lengthwise in half, so each is about 3 inches wide, and brush again lightly with oil. Place 1 scant tablespoon filling on the bottom of each strip. Fold the bottom corner to the other side to make a triangle and continue folding to the end of the strip, as if folding a flag. Place seam side down on a baking sheet. Repeat with the remaining phyllo and filling. Bake until the phyllo is golden brown, about 15 minutes. Serve warm or at room temperature.

Pirozhki

About 48 dumplings

The name for these little dumplings comes from the word pir, *meaning "feast." They are found everywhere in Russia.*

In a large bowl, combine and let stand until the yeast is dissolved:

1 envelope (2¼ teaspoons) active dry yeast
¼ cup lukewarm water

Add:

1 cup milk, at room temperature
6 tablespoons (¾ stick) butter, softened
2 large eggs, at room temperature
1 tablespoon sugar
1 teaspoon salt

Mix well, then make a soft dough by adding:

4 to 5 cups all-purpose flour

Turn out the dough onto a floured surface and knead until smooth and elastic. Place in a greased bowl, cover, and let rise in a warm, draft-free place until doubled in volume, about 1½ hours. While the dough is rising, prepare the filling. Heat in a large skillet over medium heat:

2 tablespoons vegetable oil

Add and cook, stirring, until golden, about 7 minutes:

2 large onions, finely chopped

Add and cook, stirring occasionally, until browned, about 5 minutes:

1 pound lean ground beef

Remove from the heat and stir in:

2 hard-boiled eggs, finely chopped
2 tablespoons sour cream
2 tablespoons beef stock
2 tablespoons minced fresh dill
1 tablespoon minced fresh parsley
2 teaspoons salt
Ground black pepper to taste

Lightly oil 2 baking sheets. Punch down the dough and divide into 48 balls. Roll each ball out on a floured surface to a 3½-inch round. Place a heaping tablespoon of the filling in the center of each circle. Moisten one side of the round, fold it in half, and pinch together. Gently shape each pie into an oval. Place the pies on the baking sheets, cover, and let rise until puffy, 30 to 40 minutes. Preheat the oven to 350°F.

Lightly beat:

1 large egg

Brush the tops of the dumplings with the egg wash. Bake until golden, about 20 minutes. Serve warm or at room temperature.

RULES FOR YEAST BREADS

● Find a clean surface (2 feet square is adequate) at a comfortable height for mixing and kneading.

● Use bottled spring water if your local water is hard or overly chlorinated.

● To ensure freshness, store whole-grain flours, nuts, seeds, and other ingredients containing oil in dated airtight containers in a cool, dark place or, for longer periods, in the freezer.

● Use high-gluten bread flour whenever a recipe calls for it, especially if the dough includes nongluten products (oatmeal or cornmeal, for example) or low-gluten grains like rye. Unbleached flour is preferred.

● Let ingredients come to room temperature before mixing.

● Measure accurately.

● When the dough is kneaded sufficiently, it will be smooth and elastic, and tacky rather than sticky. Set dough aside to rise in a draft-free room at a temperature of 70° to 85°F. If the room is cold, place the bowl of dough on a rack over a pan of warm water or near (but not on) a radiator or other heat source. You may also place the bowl in an oven that has been preheated for less than 1 minute until just warmed (or in a pilot-lit oven).

● Test for proper rising by pressing two fingers gently into the dough; if indentations remain, the dough is fully risen.

● Preheat the oven (unless a cold oven is specified to increase rise) and be sure to use an oven thermometer to check your oven for temperature accuracy and hot spots.

● Rotate the baking sheets or pans in the oven during baking from top to bottom and back to front.

Masa Boats with Assorted Toppings

12 appetizer servings; 24 pieces

Snack food takes on a new meaning when you taste these Mexican classics with all their flavor and pleasingly crunchy textures. Masa boats can be filled with just about anything, from simple cheese to scrambled eggs to shredded meats, fish, and poultry. The shells are made from masa harina (the dried, powdered corn flour used to make tortillas), found in many Mexican markets and large supermarkets; they can be made a day or two in advance and kept tightly covered before their final frying and filling.

Thoroughly combine in a large bowl:

2¼ cups masa harina
1½ cups hot water

Cover and let stand for 20 minutes. Mix in (knead with your hands if desired) until thoroughly combined:

⅓ cup plus 1 tablespoon
**   all-purpose flour**
2 tablespoons solid vegetable
**   shortening or lard**
1 teaspoon baking powder

¾ teaspoon salt

Divide the dough into 12 pieces and roll each into a ball. Place on a plate and cover with plastic wrap. Heat a griddle or large skillet over medium heat until hot. Press 1 ball at a time between sheets of plastic wrap into a disk about ⅜ inch thick. Place the disks in a single layer on the hot griddle and bake until lightly browned but still soft in the middle, about 2 minutes each side. Remove the browned disks to a cutting board and slice crosswise in half (as you would an English muffin). With the cooked side down, pinch a ¼-inch-high edge all around each disk, molding the pliable masa from the center. Cover tightly with plastic wrap. Have ready:

1 cup cooked or canned black
**   beans, coarsely mashed and**
**   warmed**
½ cup finely crumbled cooked
**   sausage, preferably Mexican**
**   chorizo, warmed**

About 1 cup *Salsa Fresca*, **28**
½ cup grated Mexican queso añejo
**   or Parmesan cheese**

Heat to 360°F in a large saucepan or deep skillet over medium heat:

¾ inch vegetable oil

Add 2 or 3 shells at a time to the hot oil. Fry until lightly browned but not hard, about 45 seconds. Drain on paper towels and keep warm in a 200°F oven while you fry the rest. To serve, fill each hot shell with 2 teaspoons beans, 1 heaping teaspoon sausage, a spoonful of salsa, and a generous sprinkling of cheese. Serve immediately, garnished with:

Fresh cilantro leaves

QUESO AÑEJO

Queso añejo is a hard, pungent, and salty aged goat cheese. Pecorino Romano and Parmesan make good substitutes.

HOW TO ROLL OUT PASTRY DOUGH

The secret to rolling dough is to lean into the pin rather than down on it: The goal is to enlarge the dough, not press and crush it. Start by clearing a large work surface. You can roll dough on a wood or plastic pastry board or on a marble slab (which retains cold and thus helps keep the dough from softening) or directly on a clean smooth countertop. Do not roll dough next to the oven or in a hot corner of the kitchen, or the fat will melt. If the dough has been chilled for longer than 30 minutes, let it stand until it feels firm yet pliable, like modeling clay when pressed. If too cold, the dough will crack around the edges when rolled. If the dough becomes too soft during rolling, loosen it from the work surface, slide a rimless cookie sheet beneath it, and refrigerate until it firms up.

Individual recipes specify the thickness to which to roll the dough, as well as, when necessary, its shape and size. Most often dough is rolled out into a round.

1 Flour the work surface—lightly if you are an experienced pastry maker but a bit more generously if you are starting out. Excessive flouring toughens dough, but sticking is a disaster. Place the dough in the center of the floured surface and flour the dough as well.

2 Exerting even pressure on the pin, roll the dough from the center out in all directions, stopping just short of the edge. In order to keep the dough in a circular shape, each stroke should be made in the opposite direction from the one that preceded it. You can do this by rotating the dough itself rather than by moving the pin. Be sure to check the dough for sticking by periodically sliding your hand beneath it; strew a little flour on the work surface as necessary.

3 Seal cracks and splits by pushing the dough together with your fingers. If the split reopens, your dough is probably too dry. Dab the edges of the split with cold water, overlap the edges slightly, and press firmly with your fingertips, sprinkling a little flour over the repaired area if it feels moist and sticky.

4 If the dough assumes an irregular shape, cut off the protruding piece, moisten the edge of the patch with cold water and press it over the short spot.

Empanadas

10 to 12 empanadas

These flaky meat pies are a much-loved snack all through Latin America. Although they can be filled with anything from fish to fruit, a meat filling is most common. Lard makes the most flavorful, flaky crust.

For the dough, place in a large bowl or food processor:

3 cups all-purpose flour
1½ teaspoons baking powder
1 teaspoon salt

Mix with a fork or pulse until combined. Add:

10 tablespoons (1¼ sticks) cold unsalted butter, cut into small pieces
½ cup lard or solid vegetable shortening, cut into small pieces

Cut the butter and lard into the flour mixture using a pastry blender or pulse in the food processor until the mixture resembles coarse crumbs. If using the food processor, transfer the mixture to a large bowl. Drizzle over the top:

11 to 13 tablespoons ice water

Mix gently with a fork until the flour mixture is dampened enough to gather into a ball. Shape into a flat disk, wrap tightly in plastic, and refrigerate for at least 1 hour.

For the filling, heat in a large non-stick skillet over medium heat:

1 tablespoon vegetable oil

Add:

1 medium onion, diced
2 cloves garlic, minced

Cook, stirring, until the onion is translucent, about 5 minutes. Stir in:

1 pound lean ground beef

Cook until the beef is lightly browned, about 8 minutes. Stir in:

1 cup diced peeled potatoes
1 large tomato, cored and chopped

¼ cup raisins (optional)
¼ cup coarsely chopped pitted green olives (optional)
1 teaspoon dried oregano
½ teaspoon salt
½ teaspoon ground black pepper
¼ teaspoon dried thyme

Cook, covered, over medium heat until the potatoes are tender, about 10 minutes. Uncover the pan, increase the heat to medium-high, and cook briefly to evaporate any pan juices. Remove from the heat and let cool completely.

Preheat the oven to 400°F.

To shape the empanadas, roll out the dough ⅛ inch thick on a lightly floured surface. Cut 6-inch rounds from the dough. (You will have to reroll the scraps to get 10 to 12 rounds.) Spoon about ¼ cup of the filling onto one side of each round. Moisten the edges of the rounds with water, fold each one in half, and press the edges together to completely enclose the filling. Use the tines of a fork to decoratively seal the edges. Place 2 inches apart on a baking sheet. Mix together and brush over the tops of the empanadas:

1 large egg, lightly beaten
1 tablespoon milk
Pinch of salt

Bake until nicely browned, about 15 minutes. Let cool slightly on a rack and serve warm.

Chinese Dumplings

About 20 dumplings

You can substitute ground turkey for the pork in these dumplings if you wish or, for a vegetarian version, leave out the meat and add about a cup of mung bean sprouts.

Combine in a large bowl:

2½ cups finely chopped Chinese (Napa) cabbage

1 teaspoon salt

Let stand for 30 minutes to draw out the water, then squeeze as much water as possible from the cabbage. Combine with:

8 ounces lean ground pork

1½ cups minced leeks

4 teaspoons minced garlic

1 tablespoon soy sauce

2½ teaspoons toasted sesame oil

2 teaspoons cornstarch

1½ teaspoons sake

⅛ teaspoon ground black pepper

Stir vigorously with a fork to break up the meat. If the mixture seems loose, mix in:

½ teaspoon cornstarch

Place 2 packed tablespoons of the filling in the center of each of:

20 round dumpling skins

Brush the edge with water and fold in half to make a half-moon shape, pressing out the air and sealing the edges together. If desired, form small peaks along the rounded edge using the thumb and index finger of one hand. (The straight edge of the dumpling will bend in a semicircle to conform to the shape of the pleated edge.) Place the sealed dumplings on a baking sheet lightly dusted with:

Cornstarch

Bring to a boil in a large pot over high heat:

12 cups water

Add half the dumplings, stir once or twice to prevent them from sticking, return to a boil, and boil for 7 minutes. Remove with a strainer, drain, and repeat with the remaining dumplings. Combine:

½ cup soy sauce

1 tablespoon minced garlic

and serve alongside the hot dumplings.

CHINESE CABBAGES

The so-called Chinese cabbages compare to our common cabbage as romaine lettuce compares to iceberg. Like icebergs, common cabbages have round heads with thick, crunchy, mild-tasting leaves. Like romaines, Chinese cabbages have oblong heads with thin, juicy, full-flavored leaves. The Chinese cabbage we see more and more in the supermarket is pale green Napa cabbage. These are referred to as "hearted" or "barrel shaped" to distinguish them from the long "cylindrical" shape of Michihili cabbages. You will find both Napa and Michihili at Asian markets, and their flavors and uses in cooking are much the same. Select, store, prepare, and cook as for common cabbage, but do not overcook, or their lovely flavor and texture will be destroyed. When the midrib is well developed on a leaf, remove it from the leaf, slice crosswise, and cook separately.

Fried Wontons

About 54 wontons

With a sharp knife, lightly chop until fluffy and place in a large bowl:

1 pound lean ground pork (butt or shoulder)

Shell, devein, rinse, and cut into ¼-inch dice:

½ pound medium shrimp

Press between paper towels, squeeze dry, and add to the pork. Blanch in boiling water for 10 seconds, drain, refresh in cold water, and drain again:

¾ cup water chestnuts

Press between paper towels, squeeze dry, and add to the pork. Add:

1½ tablespoons minced ginger
1½ tablespoons minced scallions, white part only

2½ tablespoons soy sauce
1 tablespoon rice wine or sake
2¼ teaspoons toasted sesame oil
1½ tablespoons cornstarch

Stir vigorously in one direction to combine. The mixture should be stiff; if not, refrigerate until firm, about 1 hour. Place a scant teaspoon of the filling in the center of each of:

54 wonton wrappers

Fold the wrapper over to form a triangle. Working from the longest edge, fold the wrapper in to a point three-quarters of the length from the opposite edge. Dip a finger in water and dab the ends of the triangle, then press the two ends together and pinch to seal. Make the

remaining wontons in the same manner. Place the finished wontons on a tray dusted with:

Cornstarch or flour

Heat a wok or deep fryer and add:

4 cups safflower or corn oil

Heat to 350°F. Add a batch of wontons and fry, stirring constantly, until the skins are golden brown and crisp, 3 to 4 minutes. Remove with a long-handled strainer and set on paper towels to drain. Bring the oil back up to 350°F and repeat the process until all the wontons have been fried, keeping the fried wontons warm in the oven. Arrange the wontons on a platter and serve with:

Plum or duck sauce
Hot mustard

ABOUT **SEAFOOD** PARTY FOODS

*F*ish and shellfish are favorites as party foods and are easy to prepare, since most of the work can be done ahead of time. No-Fail Boiled Shrimp, 78, *can be cooked a day ahead and stored in the refrigerator until ready for presentation with cocktail sauce—making shrimp cocktail. Take care to arrange the shrimp in the same direction to create a more impressive look. Dips and sauces should be made a day ahead to let the flavors blend. Use bowls, hollowed-out lemon halves, cleaned oyster shells, or whole crab shells to hold dips. You can turn broiled or grilled shrimp or scallops or any of their variations into dramatic party food by threading the seafood on skewers before grilling. Oysters and clams should be opened as close to serving time as possible.*

Smoked Trout Canapés with Horseradish Cream, 82

Clams Casino

24 clams

Fresh clams must be alive when you buy them. The shell should be intact and virtually impossible to pry open. Some hard-shell clams are farm-raised, but it is unlikely you will notice any difference.

Preheat the broiler.

Combine in a food processor or blender until smooth, about 1 minute:

4 tablespoons (½ stick) butter, softened

1 scallion, chopped

1½ tablespoons minced fresh parsley

1 tablespoon fresh lemon juice

¼ teaspoon salt

Shuck, right, and place on the half shell:

24 cherrystone clams

Spoon about 1 teaspoon of the butter mixture on top of each clam. Top with:

6 slices bacon, cooked until crisp and crumbled

Broil until the butter is bubbling, about 3 minutes. Serve hot.

SHUCKING CLAMS

To shuck raw, hold the clam in a folded dish towel and use a sturdy unsharpened paring knife to pry open the clam opposite its hinge. Scrape the meat off the bottom shell, preserving as much of the juice as you can. If you are a novice, be aware that shucking raw hard-shells is an acquired skill and requires patience. Check clams before shucking. Discard any with open shells.

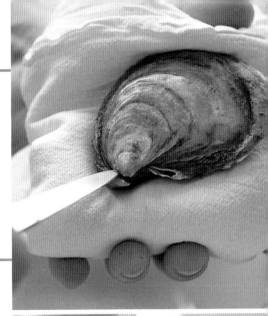

Angels on Horseback

24 oysters

Preheat the oven to 400°F.
Butter and lightly toast:

Twenty-four 2-inch bread rounds (cut from 8 pieces firm bread)

Shuck, above, and remove from shell:

24 medium oysters

Cut crosswise in half:

12 slices bacon

If desired, spread one side of the bacon lightly with:

Anchovy paste

Wrap a half slice of bacon, anchovy side in, around each oyster and secure with toothpicks. Place on a baking sheet. Bake until the bacon is crisp, about 10 minutes. Drain on paper towels. Place the oysters on the toasts and sprinkle with:

3 tablespoons minced fresh parsley

Serve immediately.

Oysters Rockefeller

24 oysters

Preheat the oven to 450°F.
Shuck, above, and place on the half shell:

24 medium oysters

Combine in a food processor just until minced, about 30 seconds:

1½ cups well-drained cooked spinach

⅓ cup fresh breadcrumbs

¼ cup chopped scallions

2 tablespoons crumbled cooked bacon

2 teaspoons chopped fresh parsley

½ teaspoon salt

4 drops hot red pepper sauce

Add:

3 tablespoons olive oil or butter, softened

1 teaspoon anisette liqueur

Process for 10 seconds more. Spoon 1 heaping teaspoon of the spinach mixture over each oyster. Sprinkle a baking sheet liberally with:

Coarse salt

Nestle the oysters into the salt to steady them. Bake until plumped, about 10 minutes, then broil until the tops are browned, about 2 minutes. Serve hot.

No-Fail Boiled Shrimp

12 to 15 appetizer servings

If you are grilling, broiling, or boiling shrimp, consider cooking them in their shells, for it protects the meat from drying out and helps them retain maximum flavor. If you wish, prepare the shrimp in plain water.

In a large saucepan, combine:

10 cups water

2 celery stalks, cut into 2-inch lengths

1 medium onion, cut into eighths

1 small lemon, quartered

½ bunch fresh parsley

8 black peppercorns

2 bay leaves

1 tablespoon salt

½ teaspoon ground red pepper

Bring to a boil, reduce the heat, and simmer, uncovered, for 10 minutes. Strain the liquid and return it to the pan. Add:

2 pounds shrimp, any size, fresh or frozen, preferably in their shells for best flavor

Return the liquid to a boil, reduce the heat, and simmer, uncovered, for 2 minutes exactly. Drain the shrimp, remove to a platter, and let cool. Set out one or more of the following for dipping:

Cocktail Sauce, right

Sauce Rémoulade, 80

Tartar Sauce, below

Cocktail Sauce

About 1 cup

This makes a lively dunking sauce. For a more contemporary sauce, add finely chopped cilantro, red onions, green chili peppers, and/or lime juice.

Stir together well in a small bowl:

½ cup ketchup

½ cup chili sauce

¼ cup finely grated horseradish

Stir in:

Hot red pepper sauce to taste

Fresh lemon juice to taste

Serve at room temperature.

Tartar Sauce Made from Blender Mayonnaise

About 1 cup

Making sauce in a blender or food processor is practically foolproof. Beat 1 egg well with a fork to blend the yolk and white, let it settle a few seconds, then measure. This recipe can easily be doubled, in which case, use the entire beaten egg.

To make Blender Mayonnaise, combine in a blender or food processor with plastic blade in place:

2 tablespoons well-beaten egg

1 large egg yolk

¼ teaspoon dry or Dijon mustard

Process on high speed until well blended, about 5 seconds in a blender, 15 seconds in a food processor fitted with the plastic blade, 30 seconds in a food processor fitted with the steel blade. Scrape down the sides, then sprinkle the mixture with:

1 teaspoon fresh lemon juice and/or white wine vinegar or rice vinegar

¼ teaspoon salt

Process for about 2 minutes in a blender, 15 seconds in a food processor fitted with the plastic blade, 7 to 8 seconds in a food processor fitted with the steel blade. Have ready in a small spouted measuring pitcher:

¾ cup oil, at room temperature

With the machine running, add the oil in the thinnest possible stream. After about one-third of the oil has been added—the mixture will have swollen and stiffened—add the oil in a slightly thicker stream. Stop the machine when all has been added and scrape down the sides and around the blade, mixing in any unabsorbed oil.

To make Tartar Sauce, stir in:

1 tablespoon minced scallions or onions or shallots

1½ teaspoons minced sour gherkins or dill pickles

1½ teaspoons drained capers

1½ teaspoons drained sweet pickle relish or minced sweet pickles (optional)

Heighten the flavors with:

A dash or two of fresh lemon juice or hot red pepper sauce

Sprinkle with:

1 tablespoon minced fresh parsley

1 tablespoon finely snipped fresh chives

Serve immediately, or refrigerate in a covered jar for 1 to 2 days.

Opposite: No-Fail Boiled Shrimp with (front to back) Tartar Sauce, above; Cocktail Sauce, above; Sauce Rémoulade, 80

Baked Honey Shrimp

12 to 15 appetizer servings

Mix together in a small bowl:

1 tablespoon chopped fresh parsley
1 teaspoon grated lemon zest

Cover and refrigerate. Whisk together in a medium bowl:

Juice of 2 lemons
½ cup olive oil
2 tablespoons soy sauce

2 tablespoons honey
2 tablespoons Cajun seasoning
1 tablespoon chopped fresh parsley
¼ teaspoon ground red pepper

Add to the bowl:

2 pounds large shrimp, peeled and deveined

Toss well, cover, and refrigerate for

1 hour, stirring occasionally. Preheat the oven to 450°F. Transfer the shrimp to a baking pan large enough to hold them in 1 layer. Bake the shrimp until firm, 8 to 10 minutes. Sprinkle with the parsley mixture and serve with:

Sliced French bread

Beer-Batter Shrimp

12 to 15 appetizer servings

Frying is a perfect way to cook shrimp because the succulent juices remain sealed inside the crisp crust. A simple squeeze of lemon juice adds the perfect acid balance to any fried seafood, but richer sauces can be used as well, such as Rémoulade, right, or Cocktail Sauce, 78.

Peel, leaving the tails on, and devein:

2 pounds medium shrimp

Open the shrimp down the back without cutting all the way through, then press flat. Stir together in a large bowl:

1 cup all-purpose flour
2 teaspoons salt
1 teaspoon baking powder

½ teaspoon ground red pepper

Whisk in:

¾ cup beer
½ cup milk
2 large eggs

Add the shrimp and let stand for 30 minutes. Heat in a deep fryer or deep, heavy pot to 365°F:

3 cups vegetable oil

Remove the shrimp 1 at a time from the batter and fry in small batches, turning twice to ensure that they are golden brown and crispy, about 4 minutes total. Using tongs, remove the shrimp to paper towels to drain. Serve as is or with:

Sauce Rémoulade, right

Sauce Rémoulade

This French classic is marvelous with vegetables, cold meats, poultry, and shellfish.

Prepare:

Blender Mayonnaise, 78

Stir in:

1 hard-boiled egg, finely chopped
1 tablespoon minced cornichons or sour gherkins
1 tablespoon drained capers
1 tablespoon chopped fresh parsley
1½ teaspoons chopped fresh tarragon
1 small clove garlic, minced
½ teaspoon Dijon mustard

Season to taste with:

Salt and ground black pepper

Molasses-Glazed Shrimp and Mango Skewers

4 appetizer servings

Be sure you wait until the last 30 seconds to brush the glaze on the skewers, or the sugar in the molasses will burn.

Prepare a medium-hot charcoal fire. Stir together in a small bowl:

¼ cup molasses

1 to 3 teaspoons red pepper flakes

Juice of ½ lime

Thread alternately onto thin metal or wooden skewers:

16 medium shrimp, peeled and deveined

1 ripe mango, peeled, pitted, and cut into 16 large chunks

Grill until the shrimp are opaque all the way through and the mangoes are slightly browned, 3 to 4 minutes each side. During the last 30 seconds of cooking, brush the shrimp and fruit generously on both sides with the glaze. Remove from the grill and serve immediately.

HOW TO CUT UP A MANGO

Mangoes are usually shipped under-ripe, as they ripen well after picking. Ripen them uncovered at cool room temperature out of the sun, turning occasionally; at warmer temperatures, they may ripen too quickly and the flavor may be altered. Mangoes can be oval or round.

1 To peel an oval or round mango, score the skin lengthwise in quarters and pull off the peel.

2 To cut up an oval mango (shown right), with a sharp serrated knife, slice down either side of the pit, which is about ½ inch thick, removing two thick pieces. Cut the remaining flesh from the pit. Cut the flesh as desired.

To cut up a round mango, working on one side at a time, cut the fruit down to the pit in slices or cubes, slide the knife down underneath, and cut the pieces free of the pit. Repeat on the other side.

Cajun Popcorn

12 to 15 appetizer servings

This recipe can be made with clams, oysters, baby shrimp, or, as it is traditionally done in Louisiana, with crayfish. In Louisiana the shells are sometimes left on, adding more crunch. These baby shrimp can be scooped up and eaten as easily as a handful of popcorn, so make sure you have plenty.

Stir together in a medium bowl:

1 cup all-purpose flour

1 teaspoon sugar

1 teaspoon salt

½ teaspoon onion powder

½ teaspoon garlic powder

½ teaspoon ground white pepper

½ teaspoon ground black pepper

½ teaspoon ground red pepper

½ teaspoon dried thyme

Make a well in the center. Gradually pour into the well, whisking constantly:

1½ cups milk

2 large eggs, lightly beaten

Let stand for 30 minutes. Meanwhile, heat to 365°F in a deep fryer or deep, heavy pot:

2 cups vegetable oil

Stir into the batter:

2 pounds baby Gulf shrimp, peeled

Remove with a slotted spoon and lightly toss with:

2 cups dry unseasoned bread-crumbs or fine cornmeal

Immediately add to the hot oil in batches and fry until crisp and lightly browned, 2 to 3 minutes. Remove with a slotted spoon to paper towels. Serve immediately with:

Garlic Mayonnaise, 50

Vietnamese Summer Rolls

4 to 6 appetizer servings

If the rice paper you are using is especially fragile and is tearing, use 2 sheets for each summer roll. Immerse them as directed, then overlap 2 sheets in the middle by 4 inches.

Bring to a rapid boil in a medium saucepan:

4 cups water

1 bundle Japanese somen noodles (about 2½ ounces), broken in half

Boil until the noodles are just firm to the bite, about 2 minutes. Use tongs or a slotted spoon to remove the noodles to a colander; rinse with cold water. Add to the still-boiling water:

16 medium shrimp, in their shells

Boil until they turn pink and float to the surface, about 2 minutes. Drain in a colander, refresh with cold water, then peel and cut lengthwise in half. Rinse with cold water to remove the veins and drain on paper towels. Place the noodles and shrimp on a small baking sheet along with:

4 large leaves red-leaf or Boston lettuce, torn lengthwise in half and central ribs removed

1 large carrot, shredded

1 cup bean sprouts

½ cup fresh mint leaves

½ cup fresh cilantro leaves

16 chives

Lay out and cover with a damp dish towel:

Eight 12-inch round sheets rice paper

Lay a damp dish towel in front of you and have a large bowl of hot water (115° to 120°F) at hand. Dip 1 sheet of rice paper into the hot water, being sure to immerse it completely. It will immediately become pliable. Quickly remove it and place on the towel. Place a piece of lettuce along the bottom edge of the rice sheet about 2 inches from the edge. Top the lettuce with one-eighth of the cooked noodles, carrots, sprouts, mint, cilantro, and chives, then with 4 shrimp halves. Fold the sides of the rice paper over the filling, then roll up tightly into a neat cylinder. Set seam side down on a large platter and cover with a damp towel to keep moist. Repeat with the remaining rice paper and filling ingredients. To serve, cut each roll crosswise into 4 even pieces (opposite). Serve immediately, or the rice paper will toughen up. Pass for dipping:

Southeast Asian Peanut Dipping Sauce, right

Southeast Asian Peanut Dipping Sauce

About 1⅔ cups

A simple, spicy sauce.

Heat in a small saucepan over medium heat:

2 teaspoons vegetable oil

Add and cook, stirring, for 5 seconds:

4 cloves garlic, finely chopped

1 small fresh chili pepper, seeded and minced

Add and cook, stirring, until thickened, about 4 minutes:

1 cup water

¼ cup soy sauce

⅓ cup chunky peanut butter, preferably unsweetened

1 teaspoon packed light brown sugar, or to taste

3 tablespoons chopped unsalted roasted peanuts (optional)

Remove from the heat and stir in, if desired:

1 tablespoon finely chopped fresh mint leaves

Serve warm or at room temperature. This sauce will keep, covered and refrigerated, for up to 1 week.

Smoked Trout Canapés with Horseradish Cream

About 75 small canapés

Using a vegetable peeler, cut lengthwise stripes into:

2 English cucumbers

Cut the cucumbers into seventy-five ¼-inch-thick slices. Stir together:

½ cup sour cream

4 teaspoons drained horseradish

Dollop about ¼ teaspoon of the horseradish cream on the center of each cucumber slice. Divide among the cucumber slices:

8 ounces boneless smoked trout, skinned and broken into small pieces about the size of almonds

These can be stored for up to 3 hours in the refrigerator, lightly covered with dampened paper towels. Garnish each canapé with:

1 tiny sprig fresh dill

Serve on a tray, garnished with:

Lemon wedges

ABOUT
CHICKEN
PARTY FOODS

*C*hicken party foods can be passed on trays with small dipping bowls if there is a sauce or served in paper-lined baskets on the table for a casual affair. Serve with more than one dip or sauce for variety. From Honey-Mustard Dipping Sauce, 103, to Creamy Blue-Cheese Dressing, 86, guests will enjoy choosing their favorite sauce from your party table. For chicken wings, some cooks prefer to substitute the lower-fat chicken "tenders" (breast pieces), 89, though these are less flavorful. If you skewer them after cooking, they make an elegant presentation.

Chicken Fingers, 89, with (left to right) Creamy Blue-Cheese Dressing, 86; Honey-Mustard Dipping Sauce, 103; Southeast Asian Peanut Dipping Sauce, 82

Buffalo Chicken Wings

About 24 pieces

These were invented at the Anchor Bar in Buffalo, New York, in 1967, and have now attained near-legendary status around the country. They are traditionally served with crisp celery sticks and blue-cheese dressing.

Preheat the oven to 350°F.

Remove and discard the wing tips (or save them for stock) from:

1½ pounds chicken wings

Separate each wing into 2 pieces at the joint; trim excess fat and skin. Stir together on a plate:

⅓ cup all-purpose flour

1 teaspoon salt

½ teaspoon ground black pepper

Coat the wings with the flour mixture and shake off the excess. Heat over medium heat in a deep fryer or deep, heavy pot to 375°F (until a corner of a wing held in the oil makes a lively sizzle):

3 cups vegetable oil

Add as many wings as will fit in a single layer without crowding; fry, turning once, until golden brown and cooked through, about 10 minutes. Drain the fried wings on paper towels and keep warm on a baking sheet in the oven. Repeat with the remaining wings. Heat in a small saucepan over low heat until foaming:

3 tablespoons butter

Remove from the heat and stir in:

2 tablespoons red wine vinegar

2 tablespoons hot red pepper sauce, or to taste

Transfer the wings to a large mixing bowl, pour the sauce over the wings, and toss until evenly coated. Taste and adjust the seasonings. Serve hot with:

Celery sticks

Creamy Blue-Cheese Dressing, right

Creamy Blue-Cheese Dressing

About 2 cups

Puree in a food processor or blender until smooth:

1 cup *Blender Mayonnaise, 78*

½ cup sour cream

¼ cup finely chopped fresh parsley

1 to 2 tablespoons fresh lemon juice or red wine vinegar

1 teaspoon minced garlic

6 dashes of Worcestershire sauce

Salt and ground black pepper to taste

Pinch of ground red pepper, or to taste

Add and process to the desired consistency:

4 ounces blue cheese

Taste and adjust the seasonings. Use immediately or cover and refrigerate.

Deviled Chicken Wings

About 24 pieces

Preheat the oven to 400°F. Grease a large baking sheet with:

2 tablespoons vegetable oil

Remove and discard the wing tips (or save them for stock) from:

1½ pounds chicken wings

Separate each wing into 2 pieces at the joint; trim excess fat and skin. Stir together in a large bowl until smooth:

½ cup honey

3 tablespoons whole-grain mustard

2 tablespoons Dijon mustard

1 tablespoon cider vinegar

Combine on a plate:

⅔ cup dry unseasoned breadcrumbs

1 teaspoon dried thyme

½ teaspoon ground red pepper, or more to taste

Toss the wings in the honey mixture.

Add 1 at a time to the crumb mixture and turn to coat completely, shaking off the excess.

Spread the wings on the prepared baking sheet. Bake, shaking the pan twice during the cooking or turning the wings with tongs, until the wings are well browned and crispy, 20 to 30 minutes. Serve hot or at room temperature.

Caribbean Style Chicken Wings

About 40 pieces

Prepare a medium-hot charcoal fire or preheat the broiler. Remove the wing tips (or save them for stock) from:

3 pounds chicken wings

Separate each wing into 2 pieces at the joint; trim excess fat and skin. Sprinkle the wing pieces with:

Salt and ground black pepper to taste

Grill or broil, turning once or twice, until golden brown, about 6 minutes. Remove to a large bowl. Add:

Juice of 3 limes

¼ cup olive oil

¼ cup chopped fresh cilantro

1 tablespoon ground cumin

1 tablespoon ground coriander

1 teaspoon minced garlic

5 to 10 dashes of hot red pepper sauce

Mix so the wings are well coated. Taste and adjust the seasonings. Serve warm or at room temperature.

Lemon Rosemary Chicken on Skewers

About 16 pieces

Cubed chicken breast is marinated, skewered, then broiled or grilled. When grilling, make sure to cover the exposed skewers with foil, or they will burn. Alternatively, cook the chicken unskewered, and skewer it afterward to serve it. If you prefer more of a glaze, you can sauté the marinated chicken in a pan with a little oil, then skewer the pieces afterward. Grilled or sautéed pieces of fruit or vegetables can be added to the skewers. For another skewered chicken dish, prepare Beef Satay, 94, using chicken.

Stir together in a medium bowl:

3 tablespoons olive oil

2 tablespoons fresh lemon juice

2 teaspoons grated lemon zest

1 teaspoon chopped fresh rosemary

1 teaspoon minced garlic

½ teaspoon salt

¼ teaspoon ground black pepper

Cut into 16 pieces by cutting each half into 8 pieces:

1 boneless, skinless chicken breast

Add the chicken to the marinade and stir to coat. Cover and refrigerate for 1 to 2 hours.

When you are ready to cook, prepare a medium-hot charcoal fire or preheat the broiler.

Thread the chicken pieces onto 16 skewers, covering the exposed wood with aluminum foil. Grill or broil just until cooked through, about 2 minutes on each side. Serve hot or at room temperature.

Chicken Liver Pâté

8 servings

The technique for this pâté differs slightly from that used in classic pâtés in that the liver is cooked and then pureed. The pâté is bound with heavy cream and butter and does not require further cooking or lengthy weighting down.

Cut into small pieces and place in the freezer:

8 tablespoons (1 stick) butter

Melt in a large skillet over medium-low heat:

2 tablespoons butter

Add:

2 large shallots, finely chopped

Cook until softened, 2 to 3 minutes. Add:

1 small Golden Delicious apple, peeled, cored, and grated

Cook, stirring constantly, until softened, about 3 minutes. Remove to a food processor. Rinse and pat dry:

1 pound chicken livers, trimmed and halved

Heat in the same skillet until the foam subsides:

1 tablespoon butter

Add the chicken livers and season with:

Salt and ground black pepper to taste

Sauté over high heat until brown on the outside but still pink in the center, about 2 minutes each side. Remove the pan from the heat. Pour in:

3 tablespoons Calvados or Cognac

If using electric heat, ignite with a match; if using gas heat, tilt the pan to catch the flame. Return the pan to the heat and swirl until the alcohol has burned off. Remove to the food processor with the apple mixture. Add:

2 tablespoons heavy cream

Process until smooth. With the machine running, drop the pieces of the cold butter 1 at a time down the feed tube. Taste and adjust the seasonings. Scrape into a small crock or bowl and smooth the top with a spatula. Press plastic wrap directly on the surface and refrigerate until firm, at least 2 hours. Serve cold or at room temperature.

Chicken Fingers

6 to 8 servings

Although you can purchase chicken tenders at most markets, we recommend cutting them at home, right.
Whisk together in a large bowl:

½ cup milk
1 large egg
1 tablespoon vegetable oil
1 tablespoon water
Stir together on a plate:
½ cup dry seasoned breadcrumbs
½ cup cornmeal
½ cup all-purpose flour
1 teaspoon salt
½ to 1 teaspoon ground red or
    black pepper
Coat in the milk mixture:
1 pound chicken tenders
Roll the tenders 1 at a time in the crumb mixture. Place in a single layer on a baking sheet. (At this point, the chicken can be refrigerated for several hours before frying.) Heat in a deep fryer or large deep, heavy pot to 375°F:

2 inches vegetable oil
Place a few tenders in the oil so the pan is not crowded and cook until golden brown, 2 to 3 minutes on each side. Drain on paper towels. Fry the remaining tenders and drain. Serve warm or at room temperature with any of the following sauces and dips:
Southeast Asian Peanut Dipping Sauce, 82
Creamy Blue-Cheese Dressing, 86
Pesto Sauce, 44
Mango Salsa, 29
Honey-Mustard Dipping Sauce, 103
Italian tomato sauce
Ranch dressing

Tandoori Chicken Fingers

6 servings

In Indian cooking, "tandoori" refers to food that is cooked in a tandoor, a fiercely hot, charcoal-fired vertical oven. The spices in this recipe give the chicken an Indian flavor. You can cut chicken tenderloins from whole breasts, right.
Toast in a heated skillet over medium heat until a shade darker and fragrant, 1 to 2 minutes:
2 teaspoons cumin seeds
2 teaspoons coriander seeds
1 small dried red chili pepper
Grind in a spice mill or clean coffee grinder. Heat in a large, heavy skillet over medium-high heat until hot but not smoking:
3 tablespoons canola or other
    vegetable oil
Add:

2 tablespoons minced peeled fresh
    ginger
Cook, stirring, until fragrant, for about 30 seconds.
Add:
1 pound chicken tenderloins
¼ teaspoon salt
Cook, stirring occasionally, for 2 minutes. Add:
2 tablespoons water
Reduce the heat, cover, and simmer until the chicken is cooked through and the water has evaporated, about 8 minutes. (If water remains in the pan, remove the chicken, boil away the juices, and return the chicken to the pan.) Add the ground toasted spices and stir to coat the chicken. Serve hot.

HOW TO CUT CHICKEN TENDERLOINS AND TENDERS

Tenderloins, the long, thin pieces of meat that lie beneath either side of a chicken breast, and "tenders," the strips cut from boneless, skinless chicken breast, can be expensive to purchase from supermarkets. You may prefer to bone and skin whole chicken breasts yourself, pulling off the tenderloins. If a recipe calls for tenders, cut the tenderloins into strips.

1 Peel off the skin with your fingers. Locate the wishbone at the wide end of the breast and scrape it free from the flesh with the tip of a paring knife.

2 Place the breast skinned side up and press down firmly with the heel of your hand to break the breastbone. Turn the breast over. Using the point of the knife, cut around the shoulder bones attached to the breastbone at the wide end of the breast and remove them. Free the breastbone and cartilage from the flesh with your fingers, then pull both out. Slip your fingers or knife beneath the rib bones and work them free of the flesh. Cut the breast in half at the breastbone line, then trim any ragged edges.

3 Place each breast half skinned side down and pull the thick end of the tenderloin away from the breast. Remove the long white tendon that runs through each tenderloin by holding the tip of the tendon down and scraping against the tendon with a knife until it detaches from the flesh. The tenderloins are ready to use in a recipe. The rest of the chicken breast can be cut into tenders.

Chicken Dumplings

About 60 dumplings

The dumplings can be made in advance and frozen in the soy mixture. Thaw, reheat, and thicken the sauce with cornstarch as directed.

Warm in a small skillet over medium heat:

1½ teaspoons vegetable oil

Add and cook until softened but not browned:

1 small clove garlic, minced

Let cool, then remove to a food processor. Add:

10 ounces boneless, skinless chicken breasts

10 ounces boneless, skinless chicken legs or thighs

Process just enough to chop the meats. Add:

2 tablespoons shiro miso (light fermented bean paste)

1 large egg yolk

Process just until smooth. Sprinkle in:

2 tablespoons all-purpose flour

Process to blend well. To make the poaching liquid, bring to a boil in a wide saucepan:

8 cups water

1 tablespoon sake

In a second wide saucepan, combine and gently simmer:

2 cups water

¾ cup soy sauce

⅓ cup sugar

¼ cup sake

2 tablespoons mirin

Moisten your hands with cold water and form the chicken mixture into ¾-inch balls. Drop a half or a third of the dumplings into the poaching liquid. Simmer until the dumplings rise to the surface, about 1½ minutes. Remove with a slotted spoon to the simmering soy mixture and simmer for 5 minutes. Remove to a plate or bowl and repeat with the remaining dumplings. Just before serving, thicken the soy mixture with a paste made from:

3 tablespoons cornstarch

⅓ cup cold water

Serve the dumplings hot or at room temperature with the sauce.

MISO

Miso, a fermented paste made from soybeans, comes in a variety of colors (from white to yellow to red) and textures (smooth or chunky), depending on the length of fermentation and the addition of grains such as barley or rice. As a general rule, the darker the miso, the longer it has been fermented and the stronger and saltier it will taste. Lighter miso, fermented for a shorter period, is sweeter. Shiro miso, which is often used in soups and delicately flavored dishes, falls into this category. Shiro miso has a fine texture and sweet flavor. Barley miso, on the other hand, is earthy and well aged. Although miso rarely spoils, it loses its flavor after a few months. Keep opened containers in the refrigerator.

ABOUT **MEAT** PARTY FOODS

*M*ost of us think of red meat primarily as a featured ingredient in main courses. Served in smaller portions, however, beef, pork, and lamb make highly satisfying little party dishes.

The key to success with any of these ingredients lies in quality, quantity, and preparation. From sirloin steak to baby back ribs, fresh pork sausages to boneless leg of lamb, the best meats bought from full-service butchers will ensure that the dishes you prepare make the best impression. The amount you need per serving will be a third or less of what you would ordinarily use for a main course. Cutting up or otherwise forming the meat into bite-sized pieces makes it easy to serve from buffet platters or passed trays.

A broad variety of seasonings, sauces, dips, and other accompaniments can add a final touch to meat party foods. Choose complementary vegetable dishes and breads or crackers to round out the party menu.

From top: Stuffed Grape Leaves, 105; Ham Rolls with Asparagus and Honey Mustard, 103

Beef and Scallion Rolls (Negi Maki)

About 30 rolls

Freeze for 20 minutes to make slicing easier:

1¼ pounds boneless beef sirloin steak, trimmed of fat

Meanwhile, trim and cut into 2-inch lengths, then divide into 15 bundles:

7 to 8 scallions

Cut the beef into 15 very thin slices. Place each slice between 2 sheets of plastic wrap and pound lightly with the bottom of a small skillet to an even thinness. (If the beef should tear, patch it with another piece on top.) Roll a piece of beef snugly around each scallion bundle, wrapping it 2 to 3 times. Secure the roll by threading a wooden toothpick lengthwise through the meat. Heat in a large skillet over high heat:

1½ tablespoons vegetable oil

Add the rolls seam side down and sear. Once the seams have sealed, turn and brown the rolls on all sides. After about 1 minute, when the beef has changed color, add:

2 tablespoons sake
2 tablespoons soy sauce
1 tablespoon sugar

Reduce the heat slightly and cook for 1 minute, shaking the pan to keep the rolls from sticking. Remove from the heat and let cool slightly. To remove the toothpicks, twist in place, then pull out gently. Reduce the sauce over high heat to 2 tablespoons. Just before serving, return the rolls to the skillet over high heat and shake to glaze them with the sauce. Slice each roll crosswise in half and serve warm (opposite).

Beef Satay with Peanut Sauce

6 to 8 appetizer servings

You can substitute strips of boneless chicken breast for the beef in this recipe. Grill the chicken longer than the beef, about 3 minutes each side. Before removing the satay from the grill, cut into one of the pieces of chicken to be sure it is cooked through.

Process in a blender or food processor until smooth:

½ cup canned unsweetened coconut milk
⅓ cup minced shallots
2 tablespoons packed brown sugar
2 tablespoons soy sauce
1 tablespoon minced garlic
1 teaspoon ground cumin
1 teaspoon ground coriander

Place in a shallow dish:

1 pound boneless beef sirloin, cut across the grain into strips about 3 x 1½ inches

Add the marinade, toss to coat the beef strips thoroughly, cover, and let stand for 1 hour at room temperature or refrigerate for up to 24 hours.

Prepare a medium-hot charcoal fire or preheat the broiler.

Whisk together in a medium saucepan:

1 cup canned unsweetened coconut milk
½ cup creamy peanut butter
4 teaspoons packed light brown sugar
1 tablespoon fish sauce
1 tablespoon soy sauce

1 tablespoon canned Thai Massaman curry paste
½ teaspoon curry powder

Whisk in thoroughly:

½ cup hot water

Simmer, stirring occasionally, over low heat until the flavors are well blended, 15 to 20 minutes. Stir in:

2 teaspoons fresh lime juice

Keep warm while you cook the meat. Thread a 6-inch-long bamboo skewer through each strip of meat. Lightly brush the skewered meat on both sides with:

Vegetable oil

Grill or broil, turning once, until golden brown, 2 to 3 minutes. Serve immediately, passing the warm peanut sauce for dipping.

Barbecued Kebabs

About 9 skewers

Shish kebab originated as a Turkish dish of skewered, marinated lamb grilled over a charcoal fire, but today we cube and skewer just about anything, from beef to vegetables, and call them kebabs. There is plenty of room for improvisation when assembling kebabs, but combine foods that will cook at the same rate of speed.

Prepare a medium-hot charcoal fire or preheat the broiler.

Combine:

1½ pounds lean ground beef or lamb

1 large onion, very finely minced (about 1 cup)

½ cup chopped fresh cilantro

One 2½-inch piece fresh ginger, peeled and minced (about ¼ cup)

1 large clove garlic, minced

2 tablespoons chopped fresh mint

2 serrano or jalapeño peppers, seeded and minced

1 tablespoon ground coriander

1 teaspoon ground red pepper

1 teaspoon salt

Shape the mixture with lightly oiled hands into 9 flattened sausages, about 4 inches long, 1½ inches wide, and 1 inch thick. Carefully thread a skewer through each sausage. Grill until browned and just cooked through, about 2 minutes each side, or broil on a slotted broiling tray for 3 to 5 minutes each side. Serve with (opposite):

Pita bread or naan

Raita, right

Raita (Indian Yogurt Salad)

About 1½ cups

Raita is best made and served fresh, but it can be prepared ahead and refrigerated, covered, for up to 2 hours. Place in a small bowl and stir together well:

1 cucumber, halved, seeded, and finely chopped

1 cup yogurt, or ½ cup yogurt and ½ cup sour cream

1 tablespoon finely chopped fresh mint

¼ teaspoon ground cumin

1 small jalapeño pepper, seeded and diced (optional)

Swedish Meatballs

About 90 meatballs

The trick to making authentic Swedish meatballs is to beat the ground meat with water until fluffy and smooth. Serve these as party food (enough for 12 to 16 guests) with small wooden picks or as a main course (for 6 to 8) accompanied by mashed potatoes and cranberry sauce.

Melt in a small, heavy skillet over medium-high heat:

1 tablespoon butter

Add and cook, stirring often, until soft, 1 to 2 minutes:

1 tablespoon minced onions

Remove from the heat and set aside. In the large bowl of an electric mixer, combine and let stand until soft, about 1 to 2 minutes:

⅔ cup fresh breadcrumbs

1 cup water

Add the reserved onions along with:

¾ pound lean ground beef

¾ pound lean ground pork

2 large egg yolks

1 teaspoon salt

¼ teaspoon ground black pepper

¼ teaspoon grated nutmeg

¼ teaspoon ground allspice

Beat on low speed until smooth. Turn the mixer to high speed and beat until the mixture is light in color and fluffy, about 10 minutes. Using two spoons dipped in cold water, shape the meat into 1-inch balls. Heat in a large skillet over medium heat:

4 tablespoons (½ stick) butter

Cook the meatballs in batches of about 15 to 20 at a time and brown on all sides. Remove with a slotted spoon and drain briefly on paper towels before removing to a warmed serving platter. Cover to keep warm. When all the meatballs are cooked, reduce the heat to low and add to the skillet:

2 tablespoons all-purpose flour

Cook, stirring, until lightly browned. Slowly add:

2 cups beef stock

Cook, whisking, until the gravy is thick and smooth. Strain, if desired. Pour the gravy over the meatballs and serve hot.

Grilled Five-Spice Ribs

6 to 8 appetizer servings

Peel and discard the rough outside husks, then thinly slice the tender core of:

2 stalks fresh lemon grass

Place in a blender or food processor along with:

3 tablespoons sugar
2 tablespoons chopped shallots
2 tablespoons minced garlic
2 tablespoons fish sauce
2 tablespoons soy sauce
2 tablespoons toasted sesame oil
2 tablespoons peanut oil
2 tablespoons five-spice powder
1 teaspoon chili bean paste

Process until finely pureed, then remove to a large bowl. Add:

3 pounds spareribs or baby back ribs, separated into individual ribs, rinsed, and patted dry

Toss to coat each rib thoroughly. Cover and let stand at room temperature for 1 hour or refrigerate for up to 24 hours.

Prepare a medium-hot charcoal fire or preheat the broiler.

Grill or broil the ribs, turning frequently, about 6 inches from the heat until the ribs are nicely browned and cooked through, 15 to 20 minutes. Serve immediately, sprinkled, if desired, with:

2 tablespoons sesame seeds, toasted

FIVE-SPICE POWDER

The first three ingredients in this licorice-scented brown powder are star anise, Szechuan pepper, and fennel or anise seeds. Cinnamon and cloves bring the number to five, but two more may be added, chosen from licorice root, cardamom, and ginger. To prepare the mixture yourself, mix by grinding into a powder equal amounts of the spices chosen; if you lack Szechuan peppercorns, use black peppercorns instead. You can substitute ground star anise for prepared five-spice powder.

Baby Riblets

About 32 riblets

Ask your butcher to cut whole racks of pork baby back ribs in half down the length of the rack to make riblets.

Whisk together in a bowl:

½ cup soy sauce

1 tablespoon minced peeled fresh ginger

1 tablespoon minced fresh cilantro or 1 teaspoon ground coriander

2 teaspoons minced garlic

½ teaspoon ground black pepper

¼ teaspoon coarse salt

Whisk in:

2 tablespoons peanut oil

1 tablespoon toasted sesame oil

Pour the soy marinade into a wide, shallow pan. Add and turn to coat evenly:

2 racks pork baby back ribs, halved

Marinate for at least 45 minutes at room temperature.

Meanwhile, preheat the oven to 400°F. Lay the ribs out on baking sheets. Bake until still slightly pink, about 30 minutes. Prepare a medium-hot charcoal fire or preheat the broiler. Grill or broil the ribs until they are deep brown and glazed, about 3 minutes each side. Baste with the marinade, cut into individual riblets, and serve hot.

FUEL FOR THE FIRE

Grilling has become synonymous with little pillow-shaped charcoal briquettes, available in every supermarket. Because they are not pure charcoal but rather a combination of charcoal, saw-dust, powdered scrap lumber, starch, and additives, briquettes can impart unpleasant flavors. Hardwood lump charcoal, made by burning hardwood in a closed container with very little oxygen, is worth searching out in hardware and specialty stores.

Rumaki

About 18 pieces

To prepare chicken livers for cooking, turn them into a colander, rinse lightly, and then pat dry with paper towels. If the livers are destined for a delicate sauté, you may want to remove the strings that connect the lobes. These can be assembled ahead of time and broiled just before serving. Any brand of sake is suitable for use in cooking except those labeled "Cooking Wine," which are made with inferior rice wines and may contain additives.

Trim well and cut in half:

8 ounces chicken livers, rinsed

Whisk together in a mixing bowl:

2 tablespoons soy sauce

2 tablespoons sake or dry sherry

1 tablespoon grated peeled fresh ginger

2 teaspoons light brown sugar

Add the livers and toss until coated. Cover and marinate in the refrigerator for 1 to 2 hours.

Preheat the broiler.

Lay out on a work surface:

6 thick slices bacon (about 8 ounces), cut crosswise into thirds

Lay 1 piece of chicken liver on each piece of bacon and roll up. Secure with a toothpick speared through the overlapping ends of the bacon and out the other side. Place on a broiler rack set on a drip pan. Broil 4 inches from the heat, turning once, until the bacon is crisp and the livers are cooked but still slightly pink inside, 5 to 6 minutes. Drain briefly on paper towels, transfer to a platter, and serve hot (opposite).

WATER CHESTNUT RUMAKI

36 pieces

Rinse and drain one 8-ounce can whole water chestnuts. Mix with 2 tablespoons teriyaki sauce and marinate for 20 minutes. Cut 12 thick slices bacon (about 1 pound) crosswise into thirds. Lay 1 water chestnut on each piece of bacon and roll up. Secure with a toothpick speared through the overlapping ends of the bacon and out the other side. Place on a broiler rack set on a drip pan. Broil 4 to 6 inches from the heat, turning once, until the bacon is cooked but not crisp. Drain briefly on paper towels. Serve hot on a bed of kale.

Sausages with Fresh Figs

6 appetizer servings

Figs from the June through July crop are generally the largest and most flavorful. The second crop in late summer is the most plentiful, but the quality is best for preserving and drying. Select tree-ripened figs if you can, but usually this delicate fruit is shipped unripe. Ripen figs uncovered at room temperature.

Prepare a medium-hot charcoal fire or preheat the broiler.

Simmer in salted water to cover until medium-rare in the center, about 6 minutes:

3 pounds fresh pork sausages with garlic

Drain well and brush lightly with:

Olive oil

Grill or broil, turning every 2 minutes or so, until lightly browned, 8 to 10 minutes total. Meanwhile, lightly brush:

15 ripe green figs, halved

with:

Olive oil

Grill or broil just until they begin to soften, about 3 minutes. Be careful not to overcook the figs. Place the figs and sausages on a platter and sprinkle with:

Extra-virgin olive oil

1 teaspoon aged sherry vinegar

Serve warm or at room temperature.

EXTRA-VIRGIN OLIVE OILS

These oils are the premium ones that are pressed and processed without heat or solvents. Color is no indication of quality and ranges from gold to deep green, depending upon where and with what olives the oil is made. Clouded, unfiltered oils are prized by many for their sometimes fuller flavor. Lamentably, the words "extra virgin" on the bottle do not guarantee good-tasting oil. If at all possible, sample before buying any quantity. Use extra-virgin oil for seasoning, salads, and cooking.

Pigs in a Blanket

16 pieces

This simple party food was ubiquitous at cocktail parties in decades past. But it's fast, easy, tasty, and due for a revival. In addition, kids love these and enjoy helping to roll them as well. Packaged dough allows variations on the classic—just make sure to gently push the perforations on the uncooked dough together to seal.

Preheat the oven to 375°F.
Carefully unroll:

One 8-ounce can refrigerated crescent roll dough

Separate into 4 equal rectangles, ignoring the corner-to-corner perforations. Cut each rectangle into four 3-inch-long strips. Brush each strip lightly with:

Dijon mustard

Top each strip with:

1 cocktail frank (16 franks total), drained well

Roll the dough around each frank, pushing the dough together at the ends to seal. Place the rolls seam side down on an ungreased baking sheet, about 2 inches apart. Whisk together, then brush lightly over the tops of the rolls:

1 large egg

1 tablespoon milk

Bake until the dough is puffy and golden brown, about 15 minutes. Let stand for 2 to 3 minutes, then serve with a dipping bowl of:

Honey-Mustard Dipping Sauce, opposite, or mustard

KIELBASA IN QUILTS

32 pieces

Prepare *Pigs in a Blanket, left,* substituting 1 pound kielbasa for the cocktail franks. Divide the dough into 4 rectangles and cut the kielbasa into 4 pieces. Brush the dough with the mustard, and roll each rectangle around a kielbasa section, pinching the seam together to seal. Refrigerate for 15 minutes to make slicing easier. Place seam side down, and slice each roll crosswise into 8 rounds. Place the rounds, meat side up, on an ungreased baking sheet, brush with the egg wash, and bake as directed.

Ham Rolls with Asparagus and Honey Mustard

20 to 25 pieces

Lay out on a work surface:

5 medium-thin slices smoked ham or prosciutto (about 8 ounces)

Carefully spread the slices with a thin layer of:

Honey mustard (about 2 teaspoons total)

Along one edge of each slice, lay:

1 cooked asparagus stalk

Roll the ham around the asparagus to form a long cylinder. Cover with plastic wrap and refrigerate until firm, 1 to 3 hours. When ready to serve, slice each roll crosswise into 4 or 5 pieces, about 1 inch long. Stand the slices, cut side up, on a platter, alone or with other rolled meats. Garnish with:

Orange slices
Watercress sprigs

Honey-Mustard Dipping Sauce

About ¾ cup

This simple sauce is especially good with fried chicken or fish.

Stir together well in a small bowl:

6 tablespoons honey
¼ cup Dijon mustard
Ground red pepper to taste

Serve at room temperature. This sauce will keep, covered and refrigerated, for up to 1 month.

Salami Rolls

30 pieces

If you like, instead of rolling, stack several layers of the salami on top of each other to form a "pie," then cut into wedges to serve. Sun-dried tomato pesto is available in many markets.

Process in a food processor until smooth:

4 ounces cream cheese, at room temperature
1 tablespoon sun-dried tomato pesto or chopped sun-dried tomatoes with a little of their oil (optional)

Lay out on a work surface:

15 thin slices Genoa salami

Spread the cream-cheese mixture over the salami. Roll each slice into a tube and cut crosswise in half. Stand the pieces up on a platter, alone or with other rolled meats.

Bread Sticks with Serrano Ham

12 pieces

Ask your butcher to slice the serrano ham as thin as possible.

Wrap:

12 long, thin bread sticks

with:

12 very thin slices serrano ham

Secure with toothpicks and serve at room temperature, accompanied, if you wish, with:

Extra-virgin olive oil for dipping
Dijon mustard
Roasted almonds

Lamb Brochettes with North African Spices

4 appetizer servings

Prepare a medium-hot charcoal fire. Mix well:

2 tablespoons caraway seeds

1 tablespoon ground cumin

1½ teaspoons ground coriander

1½ teaspoons ground black pepper

1 teaspoon red pepper flakes, or to taste

1 teaspoon salt

Thoroughly rub the spice mixture over:

8 ounces boneless leg of lamb, cut into ½-inch chunks (about 16 cubes)

Thread the lamb onto 4 skewers and grill until the lamb is done to your liking, 5 to 7 minutes on each side for medium-well done. Serve warm or at room temperature, accompanied, if desired, with:

Grilled pita wedges

Harissa

HARISSA

Used in North African cuisines, this fiery paste consists of toasted caraway, coriander, and cumin seeds, garlic, sweet paprika, and red pepper flakes that are finely ground and mixed with olive oil. Look for ready-made harissa in Middle Eastern markets.

Stuffed Grape Leaves

About 40 pieces

For a vegetarian version of this classic dish, omit the lamb, double the amount of rice, and add ½ cup dried currants and 2 tablespoons pine nuts to the filling mixture. Pour an additional 1 cup of liquid into the pan before cooking.

Drain:

Two 8-ounce jars grape leaves in brine

Separate the leaves in a large bowl and cover with boiling water. Let soak for 1 hour, changing the water (use cold water) twice to remove excess salt. Drain them and gently pat dry. Mix together until well combined:

1 ½ pounds lean ground lamb

1 medium onion, grated or finely chopped

½ cup finely chopped mixed fresh herbs (any combination of parsley, dill, and mint)

⅓ cup white rice

1 tablespoon salt

1 teaspoon dried thyme

Ground black pepper to taste

Line a Dutch oven or other large saucepan with several grape leaves, using the small or torn ones. To stuff the remaining leaves, place each one vein side up on a plate. Put a heaping tablespoon stuffing on the leaf near the stem end. Fold this end over the stuffing, then fold in the 2 sides and roll up the leaf like a small cigar, tucking in the edges to make a neat package. Squeeze gently and place seam side down in the prepared pan. Continue stuffing the leaves in the same manner, packing them tightly together in a single layer. Repeat with a second layer. (Leave a few leaves unstuffed.) Drizzle over the top:

3 tablespoons olive oil

Pour in:

2 cups chicken or beef stock or water

Cover the top with more grape leaves and weight with a small plate. Cover the pan and simmer over low heat until the lamb is cooked and the packages are hot, about 30 minutes. Serve hot or cold, accompanied, if desired, with:

Plain yogurt

STORING FRESH HERBS

Most fresh herbs are perishable. Store bunches in the refrigerator, their stems in water. Pack loose leaves and flowers and rhizomes in perforated plastic bags in the refrigerator or crisper.

ABOUT
PARTY DRINKS

*M*ixed drinks bestow an air of conviviality upon social occasions. On the following pages, you'll find recipes and background information for all manner of popular mixed drinks suitable to serve at a party.

Do not feel that you must have a fully stocked bar. A successful party can center on just a few different mixed drinks, such as martinis or margaritas, and suitable accompanying foods. Wine and beer are also popular, whether offered as alternatives to cocktails or in place of them. Many cocktails can also be made in "virgin" versions by simply omitting the liquor. Be sure to have on hand a selection of soft drinks, juices, and bottled waters for making mixed drinks.

From left: Champagne; Martini, 112

Cocktails

The chief virtue of cocktails is their informal quality. They loosen tongues and unbutton the reserves of the socially diffident. They may be alcoholic or non, incidentally; even the latter serve to perk up a social gathering. The origins of the word *cocktail* are unknown. One theory suggests that tavern keepers once poured odds and ends of liquors together into a bottle whose cork was stuck with a rooster's tail feather, but the word was first used in print in the nineteenth century. Cocktails are almost certainly an American invention and seem undeniably in the American spirit of improvisation.

The heyday of the cocktail lasted from the 1920s until perhaps the early 1960s. Since that time, Americans have discovered the pleasure of wine. Concurrently, both wine lovers and food writers (and occasionally chefs) have spread the fiction that even a single drink of "hard liquor" will somehow deaden the palate. This is not true, though one should of course not overdo it. But remember that cocktails are before-meal drinks. For this reason, they should be neither sweet nor overloaded with cream, in order to avoid spoiling the appetite instead of stimulating it. Mixed properly, few things can compare to a well made cocktail.

Highballs, Rocks, and Shots

The simplest ways to drink spirits are as highballs, on the rocks, or in straight shots. A highball, which some purists don't consider to be a cocktail at all, is usually defined as simply a combination of one kind of liquor and a mixer—club soda, tonic water, fruit juice, etc.—served in a tall glass with or without a simple garnish (for instance, a twist of lemon peel). "Rocks," of course, are ice cubes; drinks on the rocks are usually presented in an old-fashioned glass, sometimes with a garnish. A shot glass is a small stemless glass, holding approximately one jigger (1½ ounces) of alcohol. The idea of a drinker ordering whiskey by the shot and downing it in a single gulp suggests the Wild West, but some people like to drink straight shots of premium vodkas or shots of single-malt Scotch "neat"—that is, with neither ice nor water—and others add a splash of the latter believing it releases flavor and aroma from the whisky.

From left: water, pastis, Campari, sweet vermouth

Apéritifs

European drinking habits traditionally favor the consumption of what the French call the apéritif, or opener, in place of the cocktail. An apéritif may be as simple as a glass of Champagne or white wine, and in some countries even a beer. But there is also an entire class of herb-and-spice-flavored wine or spirit concoctions intended specifically for the purpose. The best known of these is vermouth, which is nothing more than wine with various flavorings added. Although vermouth is indispensable for making martinis and other classic cocktails, it is also very pleasant served by itself, either chilled or on the rocks. Vermouth comes in dry and sweet versions—white and red, respectively. France and Italy produce the best vermouths, though some perfectly acceptable ones are made in the United States as well. Traditionally, dry vermouth is called French and sweet vermouth Italian, but both countries make both kinds.

The most famous spirit-based apéritif, or perhaps we should say aperitivo, irreplaceable in certain cocktails, is the bright red, pleasantly bitter Campari. An apéritif "cocktail" currently popular in Italy is the Shakerato; this is simply a jigger or more of Campari agitated very vigorously with ice in a cocktail shaker, then strained into a chilled cocktail glass. If shaken correctly, it has an attractive pink foam on it and somehow has turned slightly sweet. Several other bitter apéritifs from both Italy and France are sold in America today. Pastis, popular in the south of France, is a potent anise-flavored apéritif and was formulated as a substitute for the fabled absinthe after the latter was banned. Pastis figures in some cocktails but is usually consumed over ice with water added, which turns it from clear to milky in color.

The Art of Home Bartending

Other than glasses and the gadgets designed to open various mixes, the most important pieces of equipment a home bartender can have are a cocktail shaker, or bartender's glass (with top), and a strainer, (sometimes built into the top). Many cocktails must be shaken (or stirred) with ice, then strained into another vessel. In a pinch, a clean plastic refrigerator bottle with a tight-fitting top and a kitchen sieve will produce the same effect. A standard jigger, which is a 1½-ounce measure, usually conical in shape, is also useful; some handy models are two-sided with a pony (a 1-ounce measure) as a counterbalance. Jiggers are also available in fractional sizes (¼, ½, and ¾ ounce). Many bartenders, both professionally and at home, prefer to "free pour"—that is, to splash ingredients into a cocktail shaker or glass without measuring precisely. With a bit of practice, anyone can learn to approximate a 1½-ounce pour—or increase or decrease it at will.

While no good host or hostess deliberately serves watered-down drinks, neither are you doing your guests—and the public at large—a favor by serving unasked-for "doubles" or "triples." Cocktails are often intricate formulas designed to balance elements in an agreeable way; adding too much vodka to a Bloody Mary is as misguided as putting too much salt in a stew.

Other useful additions to the home bar are a lemon peeler, a long mixing spoon, an ice bucket (with tongs), a squeezer for extracting citrus juices, an ice crusher (or heavy ice bar and

mallet), and perhaps a bitters bottle (which dispenses a drop of liquid at a time)—but none of these is essential. A blender is necessary for certain kinds of cocktails (a Piña Colada, for example). Of course, if you're going to serve wine, you'll need a good corkscrew. Although these come in many designs, we prefer the simple waiter's corkscrew, which works on the fulcrum principle—preferably it is one with a long, wide screw.

There is a trend in some restaurants and bars today to serve every kind of cocktail in the same style of glass—a kind of wine goblet. This will work in a pinch, but a stock of basic glasses of varying sizes and designs is useful for the home bartender, and sipping a drink from the proper receptacle will add to your guests' enjoyment of the portions you provide. A cocktail glass holds about 3 ounces and has a long stem flaring into a bowl, bucket, or saucer shape. An old-fashioned glass is short and squat and holds about 6 ounces. A highball glass is a tall, thinnish tumbler, generally holding 8 to 12 ounces; a collins glass is a longer, thinner version, holding 14 to 16 ounces

Sugar Syrup

A useful ingredient for many cocktails is a sugar syrup.
Boil for 5 minutes:

1 part water

2 parts sugar

Keep the sugar syrup in a bottle, refrigerated, and use as needed.

Opposite, from left: cocktail glass, highball glass, collins glass, old-fashioned glass

Gin

Gin, or at least its precursor, was invented in Holland in 1650 by a doctor who infused distilled grain spirits with juniper berries and promoted it as a curative. Dutch gin, or jenever, retains a more pronounced flavor of juniper and other herbs and spices to this day; it is usually drunk straight and chilled, and the aged jenevers elicit as much reverence as fine whiskey.

The British quickly discovered, adopted, and reformulated gin, and it is the London "dry" style that we know so well today. Gin used to have a bad reputation. It was the common favorite of poorer women and men in England, dubbed "mother's ruin," and associated with crime and public drunkenness. The "bathtub" concoctions of the Roaring Twenties also did nothing to improve its image. Recent generations, however, have recognized that this liquor, regardless of its shady past, is probably the best cocktail mixing base invented.

Martini

1 serving

A great deal has been written about this quintessential cocktail over the years, and a great deal of nonsense has been promulgated. Vermouth is not the enemy of the martini; it is its defining element. Good gin is a potent spirit with real flavor of its own, but it needs more than a suspicion of vermouth to turn it into a cocktail. Drink it straight if that's the way you like it, but don't call it a martini. A classic martini is served "straight up" in a chilled cocktail glass, though a fashion for sipping the cocktail on the rocks has developed—perhaps with the intention of muting its strength. A pitted green olive is the traditional garnish, but there are those who prefer a lemon twist. (With a small pickled onion, the martini becomes a Gibson.) A Vodka Martini, of course, is one in which vodka takes the place of gin.
For a classic martini:

Shake or stir well with ice:
1½ jiggers (2¼ ounces) gin
½ pony (½ ounce) dry vermouth
Strain into a chilled cocktail glass or over ice in an old-fashioned glass.
Add:
1 small pitted green olive
or twist over the top:
1 strip lemon peel

From left: Gimlet, Gin Fizz, Singapore Sling (all opposite)

Gimlet

1 serving

Replace the jigger of gin with vodka for a Vodka Gimlet. Substitute freshly squeezed orange juice for half of the lime juice, and you'll have an Orange Blossom.

Shake with ice:

1 jigger (1½ ounces) gin
Juice of ¼ lime

Strain into a chilled cocktail glass.

Garnish with:

1 lime wedge

Gin Fizz

1 serving

A Silver Fizz is made by beating a large egg white into the ingredients for a Gin Fizz.

Shake with ice:

1 jigger (1½ ounces) gin
Juice of 1 lime
1 tablespoon *Sugar Syrup*, 110

Strain into a chilled highball glass.

Fill with:

Club soda

Stir and serve.

Bronx

1 serving

Despite its name, this cocktail is said to have been created in Manhattan.

Shake with ice:

1 jigger (1½ ounces) gin
Dash of dry vermouth
Dash of sweet vermouth
½ pony (½ ounce) orange juice (preferably freshly squeezed)

Strain into a chilled cocktail glass and garnish with:

1 orange slice

Negroni

1 serving

Invented at the Casoni Bar in Florence, Italy, in the 1920s in honor of Count Camillo Negroni, this is one of the most elegant and sophisticated of cocktails. A lower-proof version, known as the Americano, omits the gin and adds a few ounces of soda on top, while a Campari Cocktail is a Negroni with Italian brandy substituted for the gin. Regular Campari, a closely guarded recipe, is made from herbs. It is a distinctive, bittersweet, popular Italian apéritif; sweet Campari is also available.

Pour over ice in a highball glass:

1 jigger (1½ ounces) gin
1 jigger (1½ ounces) Campari
1 jigger (1½ ounces) red Italian vermouth

Stir well. This cocktail may also be shaken with ice and strained into a chilled cocktail glass. In either case, garnish with:

1 orange slice

Singapore Sling

1 serving

Barman Ngiam Tong Boon invented this cocktail in the early 1900s at the legendary Long Bar at Raffles Hotel in Singapore. There are countless versions, the only constants being gin, cherry brandy, and grenadine. Even the formula given out by Raffles itself has varied through the years. Some formulas call for topping the glass off with club soda.

Shake well with ice:

1 pony (1 ounce) gin
½ pony (½ ounce) cherry brandy
4 ounces (½ cup or 2 jiggers and 1 pony) pineapple juice (preferably fresh)
Dash of Triple Sec
Dash of Bénédictine
Juice of ¼ lime
Dash of grenadine syrup
Dash of Angostura bitters

Pour over ice in a collins glass.

Garnish with:

1 pineapple slice
1 maraschino cherry

Tom Collins

1 serving

This was once the definitive highball. Substituting vodka for gin produces a Vodka Collins.

Shake with ice:

1 jigger (1½ ounces) gin
Juice of ½ lemon
1 tablespoon *Sugar Syrup*, 110

Strain over crushed ice in a collins or highball glass. Fill with:

Club soda

Garnish with:

1 lemon slice

Vodka

Vodka—neutral spirits distilled from grain (and occasionally from potatoes or even grapes)—is sometimes considered the perfect cocktail mixer, because it adds the kick and bite of alcohol to a drink without imposing much flavor of its own. American law, in fact, defines vodka as being "without distinctive character, aroma, taste, or color." Nonetheless, the water on which it is based (its name is Russian for "little water") and the quality and variety of the grain from which it is made have some influence on it. Vodka lovers will tell you that the better brands most definitely do have flavors of their own. There are also available an increasing number of flavored vodkas, enhanced with lemon, currants, chili peppers, and an herb known as buffalo grass, among other things, which are served straight and as cold as ice.

Bloody Mary

1 serving

This and the Screwdriver, opposite, are slightly less aggressive than most other cocktails. For this reason they are often served at brunch. When tequila takes the place of vodka in a Bloody Mary, top left, it becomes a Bloody María; made with gin, it is a Ruddy Mary. Replace half the tomato juice with chilled beef bouillon or consommé and you'll have a Bloody Bull; replace it all with beef bouillon and omit the celery salt, salt, and pepper, and the result is a Bullshot. A Bloody Mary without any alcohol is, of course, a Virgin Mary.

Shake well with ice:
1 jigger (1½ ounces) vodka
6 ounces (¾ cup or 4 jiggers)
  tomato juice (preferably fresh)
2 or 3 drops lemon juice
2 or 3 drops Worcestershire sauce
Drop of hot red pepper sauce
Pinch of celery salt
Pinch of salt
Pinch of ground black pepper
Strain over ice in a highball glass.
Garnish with:
1 small celery stalk

Moscow Mule

1 serving

This refreshing cocktail (left bottom) is said to have been invented at the now-defunct Cock 'n' Bull in West Hollywood, long frequented by Hollywood's British colony. Replacing the vodka with dark rum creates a Dark and Stormy, a popular libation on the island of Bermuda.

Pour over ice in a chilled mug or highball glass:
1 jigger (1½ ounces) vodka
Juice of ½ lime
Ginger beer to fill mug or glass
  (5 to 7 ounces)
Stir well.

Salty Dog

1 serving

This once popular variation on the screwdriver is now largely forgotten but is overdue for a revival. Without the salty rim, this drink is called a Greyhound.

Shake well with ice:

1 jigger (1½ ounces) vodka

6 ounces (¾ cup or 4 jiggers) grapefruit juice (preferably freshly squeezed)

Moisten the rim of a highball glass, then dip it in:

Coarse salt

Drop ice into the glass and strain in the drink.

Black Russian

1 serving

The name for this cocktail no doubt derives from the dramatic color that results when the very dark brown, Mexican coffee-flavored liqueur called Kahlúa is combined with good Russian vodka. To make a White Russian, stir a jigger (1½ ounces) heavy cream into a Black Russian.

Shake well with ice:

1 jigger (1½ ounces) vodka

1 pony (1 ounce) Kahlúa or other coffee liqueur

Strain over ice in an old-fashioned glass.

Screwdriver

1 serving

Folklore has it that this drink was named by oil-rig workers in the Middle East who stirred the canned cocktail with their screwdrivers. Screwdrivers are best made quickly. Top a screwdriver with ½ ounce of Galliano for a Harvey Wallbanger.

Shake well with ice:

1 jigger (1½ ounces) vodka

6 ounces (¾ cup or 4 jiggers) orange juice (preferably freshly squeezed)

Strain over ice in a highball glass.

Garnish with:

1 orange slice

VIRGIN COCKTAILS

Simple instructions for making nonalcoholic versions of several classic cocktails are given with the recipes for the alcoholic versions. Here are a couple more:

SHIRLEY TEMPLE

1 serving

For generations, this has been the first "cocktail" sampled by American children—practically none of whom, of course, ever heard of Shirley Temple, a child movie star in the 1930s. Substituting cola for ginger ale produces a Roy Rogers, named after a movie cowboy hero in the 1940s. The sweet pomegranate-like flavor of the grenadine in this drink is a hit with adults as well as children.

Stir together with ice in an old-fashioned glass:

Dash of grenadine syrup

Ginger ale to fill glass

Garnish with:

1 maraschino cherry

CRANBERRY COLLINS

1 serving

Stir together with ice in a highball glass:

4 ounces (½ cup or 2 jiggers and 1 pony) sweetened cranberry juice

Juice of ½ lemon

Fill the glass with:

Club soda

Garnish with:

1 lemon slice

Serve immediately.

Rum

As blithe and potent as gin and perhaps the most versatile of mixers after gin, rum is distilled from the juice of sugar cane or from molasses made from sugar cane. As it is produced primarily in the Caribbean and South America, it is hardly surprising that rum is the traditional alcoholic constituent of tropical fresh fruit punches. What is perhaps more surprising is that the heavier, more pungent rums (for instance, those of Jamaica) and some of the lighter ones from the French islands of Guadeloupe and Martinique can achieve great subtlety and complexity when well aged and can be served like fine brandy in a snifter. It's important to note that you don't want to waste these fine rums in mixed drinks. In general, light rums should be used for cocktails and medium-bodied or dark but young ones for punches and long drinks.

Mai Tai

1 serving

Victor "Trader Vic" Bergeron claimed to have devised this tropical classic. He mixed it up one evening at his Hinky Dinks restaurant in Oakland, California (precursor to the first Trader Vic's), and gave it to some visiting friends from Tahiti, who pronounced it "Mai tai—roa aé," said to mean "Out of this world—the best."

Shake well with ice:
1 pony (1 ounce) dark rum (preferably Jamaican)
1 pony (1 ounce) light rum
½ pony (½ ounce) curaçao (orange-flavored liqueur from the Caribbean)
½ pony (½ ounce) orgeat (almond syrup)
Dash of grenadine syrup
Juice of ½ lime
Strain into an old-fashioned glass, with or without ice.
Garnish with:
The lime shell from the juiced lime and 1 mint sprig
Or:
A small skewer of fresh fruit

Daiquiri

1 serving

This simple, elegant cocktail has declined in popularity in recent years, at least in its pure form. To make a Frozen Daiquiri, process the ingredients in a blender with 3 or 4 ice cubes until frothy and smooth. For a Banana Daiquiri, add a sliced ripe banana to the ingredients for a Frozen Daiquiri and process until frothy and smooth. Other fresh fruit (peaches, strawberries, papaya, etc., minus their peels, pits, or seeds) may be substituted for the banana.

Shake well with ice:
1 jigger (1½ ounces) dark rum
Juice of ½ lime
1 teaspoon *Sugar Syrup*, 110
Strain into a chilled cocktail glass.

Piña Colada

1 serving

Piña Coladas are best made with fresh pineapple juice. Pineapples are available year-round, which seems miraculous in the chill of winter. To make your own juice at home, peel, core, and cut into cubes 2 large ripe pineapples. Process in a blender or juicer. Whatever pulp remains can be removed with a slotted spoon before the juice is strained. If the juice seems too thick, dilute it with a little cold water. For a nonalcoholic Niña Colada, replace the rum with a dash of grenadine syrup.

In a blender, process until smooth and frothy:

1 jigger (1½ ounces) dark rum
2 jiggers (3 ounces) pineapple juice (preferably fresh)
2 ounces unsweetened coconut milk
3 or 4 ice cubes

Pour into a goblet (right) or highball glass. Garnish with:

½ slice fresh pineapple

Planter's Punch

1 serving

Planter's Punch is one of the oldest rum drinks.

Shake well with ice:

1 jigger (1½ ounces) dark rum
6 ounces (¾ cup or 4 jiggers) orange juice (preferably freshly squeezed)
Dash of grenadine syrup
Juice of ¾ lime
1 teaspoon *Sugar Syrup*, 110

Strain over ice in a highball glass. Garnish with:

1 orange slice

Cuba Libre

1 serving

Changing political events may imbue the name of this drink—Free Cuba— with varying degrees of irony, but it remains a Caribbean classic. Although any cola may be used, the drink was made originally and is indelibly associated with Coca-Cola.

Pour over ice in a highball glass:

1 jigger (1½ ounces) dark rum
6 ounces (¾ cup or 4 jiggers) cola
Juice of ½ lime

Stir and garnish with:

1 lime slice

Hot Buttered Rum

1 serving

This hot drink is perfect when the weather gets brisk. Nutmeg or cloves (the spicy, dried, rich red unopened bud of the clove tree) add great flavor to this drink.

Place in a 6- or 8-ounce mug:

1 jigger (1½ ounces) dark rum
1 teaspoon sugar
1 teaspoon unsalted butter

Fill the mug with boiling water and stir. Sprinkle the top with:

Pinch of ground nutmeg or cloves

Tequila

Mexico's tequila is currently one of the fastest-selling spirits in the United States, thanks largely to the popularity of a single cocktail—the Margarita. Tequila is distilled from the fermented sap of the blue agave plant, usually mixed with neutral spirits of various kinds. More perhaps than is the case with other "white" liquors, the quality of commercial tequila varies. Its cost is a rough measure of its worth, and there are some very good premium tequilas being sold in the United States. Technically, tequila is a specific kind of mezcal from a specific region of Mexico, and generic mezcal has long been seen as tequila's poor relation. There are now some premium mezcals being imported, however, which are superb.

Tequila Sunrise

1 serving

Pour over ice in a highball glass:

1 jigger (1½ ounces) tequila

6 ounces (¾ cup or 4 jiggers) orange juice (preferably freshly squeezed)

Stir well, then pour over the top:

Dash of grenadine syrup

Do not stir but garnish with:

1 orange slice

Margarita

1 serving

The Margarita (left) was invented either in Acapulco by a Texan named Margarita Sames, or at the bar at the Caliente Race Track in Tijuana, or at the old Tail o' the Cock restaurant in Los Angeles, or at the Kentucky Club in Juárez, or . . . Wherever it was first formulated, it seems to have been based on an earlier cocktail called the Sidecar, which is made with brandy instead of tequila and has a rim coated with sugar instead of salt. Today, it is one of the most often served of all cocktails. To make a Frozen Margarita, combine the liquors and lime juice in a blender with 4 to 6 ice cubes and blend until the ice is almost but not quite disintegrated. Strain into a chilled cocktail glass (without salt).

Shake well with ice:

1 jigger (1½ ounces) tequila

½ pony (½ ounce) Triple Sec or Cointreau

Juice of ½ lime

Moisten the rim of a chilled cocktail glass, then dip it in:

Coarse salt

Drop the lime shell into the glass and strain in the drink.

Whiskey and Whisky

There are two kinds of whisky (as it is known in Scotland and usually in Canada) and a number of kinds of whiskey (including Irish, bourbon, rye, and others). Whiskey, as we will call it inclusively for the sake of clarity, is a distilled grain spirit, whether that grain is barley, corn, or rye.

Whiskey Sour

1 serving

Shake well with ice:

1 jigger (1½ ounces) blended whiskey

Juice of ½ lemon

½ teaspoon Sugar Syrup, 110

Pour into a chilled small goblet. Garnish with:

1 lemon slice

1 maraschino cherry

Rusty Nail

1 serving

Drambuie is a liqueur based on Scotch that is sweetened with honey and flavored with herbs. It comes from Scotland.

Pour over ice in an old-fashioned glass:

1 jigger (1½ ounces) Scotch

½ pony (½ ounce) Drambuie

Stir.

Sazerac

1 serving

Invented at the old Sazerac Coffee House in New Orleans in the mid–nineteenth century, this unique cocktail was originally made with brandy instead of whiskey and with now-illegal absinthe in place of Herbsaint (an anise-flavored liquor).

Place in a chilled old-fashioned glass:

½ pony (½ ounce) Herbsaint, Pernod, or other anise-flavored liqueur

Swirl it around so that it coats the inside of the glass, then pour it out. Stir with ice:

1 jigger (1½ ounces) rye or blended whiskey

Dash of Peychaud or Angostura bitters

½ teaspoon Sugar Syrup, 110

Pour with the ice into the glass and garnish with:

1 lemon twist

Old-Fashioned

1 serving

A classic cocktail.

In an old-fashioned glass, stir together:

1 teaspoon Sugar Syrup, 110

1 teaspoon water

Dash of Angostura bitters

Add:

1 jigger (1½ ounces) blended whiskey

3 or 4 ice cubes

Garnish with:

1 orange slice

1 maraschino cherry

Manhattan

1 serving

A Rob Roy is a Manhattan made with Scotch. A Perfect Manhattan uses a dash each of dry and sweet vermouth.

Pour over ice in an old-fashioned glass:

1 jigger (1½ ounces) bourbon, rye, or blended whiskey

2 dashes of dry vermouth

Dash of Angostura bitters

Stir well. This cocktail may also be shaken with ice and strained into a chilled cocktail glass. Garnish with:

1 maraschino cherry

Mint Julep

1 serving

In a chilled highball glass or frosted silver mug, muddle (crush together with a muddler or the end of a wooden spoon):

5 or 6 fresh mint leaves

1 teaspoon Sugar Syrup, 110

Dash of cold water

Fill the glass with:

Crushed ice

Pour in:

1 jigger (1½ ounces) bourbon

Stir once and garnish with:

1 mint sprig

Brandy

To answer immediately what may well be the most asked question about brandy: All Cognac is brandy but not all brandy is Cognac. The word *brandy* comes from the Dutch *brandewijn*, meaning "burnt" (that is, distilled) wine, and as the term is commonly used, brandy is just that. Local laws allowing, it may be made anywhere that wine is made (or that wine made elsewhere is available). Cognac, the world's most famous brandy, is made in the Cognac region of France according to legally determined and closely regulated methods.

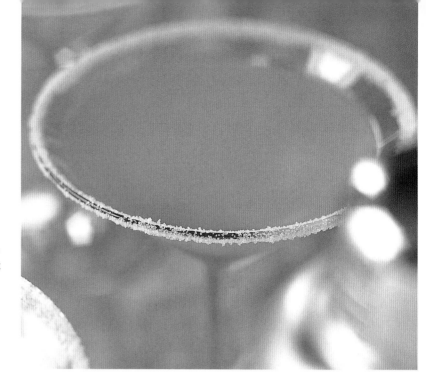

Sidecar

1 serving

The story is that this stylish cocktail was created at Harry's Bar in Paris in the 1920s at the behest of a raffish young American expatriate who rode around the city in the sidecar of a friend's motorcycle. A sidecar with Armagnac instead of Cognac has been dubbed an Armored Car. Substitute light rum for half the Cognac and lime for lemon juice, and you've got a Between the Sheets.

If you like, moisten the rim of a chilled cocktail glass and dip it in:
Sugar

Shake with ice:
1 pony (1 ounce) V.S.-quality Cognac
½ pony (½ ounce) Triple Sec
Juice of ½ lemon
Strain into the chilled cocktail glass (above).

French 75

1 serving

The original French 75 was a 75-mm French artillery piece used during World War I. This cocktail reportedly had a similar kick.
Shake with ice:
1 jigger (1½ ounces) French brandy
Juice of ½ lemon
1 teaspoon superfine sugar
Strain into a champagne flute or collins glass and fill glass with:
Chilled Champagne

Stinger

1 serving

Variations on the Stinger can be made by substituting Cognac or another liqueur or spirit for the brandy; however, the white crème de menthe is essential. Although we use a chilled cocktail glass, you can also serve a Stinger straight up in an old-fashioned glass.
Shake with ice:
1 jigger (1½ ounces) brandy
1 pony (1 ounce) white crème de menthe
Strain into a chilled cocktail glass.

Brandy Alexander

1 serving

Crème de cacao is a liqueur flavored with cacao (used to make cocoa and chocolate) and sometimes vanilla beans. Notoriously rich and sweet, Brandy Alexanders might best be served after dinner rather than before.
Shake with ice:
1 pony (1 ounce) brandy
1 pony (1 ounce) dark crème de cacao
Dash of heavy cream
Strain into a chilled cocktail glass.

Cordials

The terms "cordial" and "liqueur" usually are considered interchangeable, but the former specifically suggests considerable sweetness. Cordials usually have one predominant flavor, while liqueurs have a more intricate flavor based on several ingredients.

Grasshopper

1 serving

Shake with ice:
1 pony (1 ounce) green crème de menthe
1 pony (1 ounce) white crème de cacao
1 pony (1 ounce) half-and-half
Strain into a chilled cocktail glass.

Fuzzy Navel

1 serving

Pour over ice in a highball glass:
1 jigger (1½ ounces) peach schnapps
½ cup (4 ounces) orange juice (preferably freshly squeezed)
Stir, then garnish with:
1 orange slice

Wine Cocktails

Some of the most refreshing party drinks are made by combining wine with mixers. To make these so-called wine cocktails, you do not need to use a bottle of the highest quality. However, you should select a wine that you would enjoy drinking on its own.

White Wine Spritzer

1 serving

Combine over ice in a large wine or highball glass:
4 ounces (½ cup) chilled German or California Riesling or other semidry white wine
4 to 6 ounces (½ to ¾ cup) club soda

Champagne Cocktail

1 serving

Place in a champagne flute or saucer-type champagne glass:
1 small sugar cube
Onto the sugar cube drip:
1 or 2 drops Angostura bitters
Fill the glass with:
Chilled Champagne

Kir

1 serving

Canon Félix Kir was the mayor of the city of Dijon, in the Burgundy region of France, and a hero of the Resistance during World War II. His favorite drink was then called vin blanc cassis, *based on the good white wine of the region and another local product—black currant liqueur. Locals renamed the beverage in his honor. A Kir Royale replaces the white wine with Champagne; a Kir Cardinale uses red wine in place of white.*

Combine in a large wine glass:
6 ounces (¾ cup) chilled Mâcon Blanc or other dry white wine
Dash of crème de cassis
Stir.

Mimosa

1 serving

If you use freshly squeezed orange juice and a modest vintage French Champagne—or at least a French, Californian, Italian, or Spanish sparkling wine of good quality—this popular brunch cocktail approaches true elegance. It is also delicious made with the juice of blood oranges.

Pour into a chilled 8-ounce champagne flute or wine glass:
¼ cup (2 ounces) orange juice (preferably freshly squeezed)
Fill the glass with:
Chilled nonvintage French Champagne or other good-quality sparkling wine
Stir once.

Bellini

1 serving

This luxurious cocktail was invented at Harry's Bar in Venice. Harry's packages a Bellini mix based on fresh peaches, which is an acceptable substitute when fresh peaches are not available. Use about two tablespoons of the mix in place of a half fresh peach. For an alcohol-free Baby Bellini, replace the wine with ginger ale or a citrus-based soft drink.

In a blender, process until smooth:
½ ripe peach, peeled and pitted
Pour into a champagne flute, then fill with:
Chilled prosecco (Italian sparkling wine), Champagne, or other sparkling wine

Punches and Party Drinks

Most of the formulas in the section that follow are of the punchbowl variety. The punchbowl is an old-fashioned serving piece found less often in homes today than it once was. By virtue of its identity as a kind of communal watering hole, it tends to animate social gatherings in ways that go beyond the effects of the alcohol it might contain. If you don't have a punchbowl for your party, consider renting or borrowing one. Punches and party drinks may also be served, however, in attractive pitchers. Ideally, punch mixes should be allowed to blend for an hour or so before serving and, if served cold, should be chilled in the refrigerator before carbonated water or ice is added. Cold punches become easily diluted, so be on the alert for dilution. Ice only two-thirds of the liquid at the outset and add the remainder just before the guests come back for seconds.

Champagne Punch

20 servings

For a nonalcoholic Mock Champagne Punch, replace the brandy, rum, curaçao, and maraschino with a 750-ml bottle of cola and substitute soda water or a citrus-flavored soft drink for the Champagne. For a dramatic effect, make the Decorative Ice Ring, right.

Peel, core, slice, crush, and place in a large bowl:

3 ripe pineapples

Cover the pineapple and juice with:

1 pound powdered sugar

Let stand, covered, for 1 hour. Stir in:

½ bottle (about 1½ cups or 12 ounces) brandy
½ bottle (about 1½ cups or 12 ounces) light rum
2 jiggers (3 ounces) curaçao
2 jiggers (3 ounces) maraschino
Juice of 12 lemons

Let stand for 4 hours. Transfer to a punch bowl with:

1 block ice

Stir to blend and chill. Just before serving, pour in:

4 bottles (750 ml each) chilled Champagne

Decorative Ice Ring

Distilled water results in a clearer, less cloudy ice. If using tap water, be sure to allow it to sit in the refrigerator for at least an hour to help to prevent cloudiness. Or, stir well in a bowl 4 or 5 times during a 10- to 15-minute period to break up and expel the air bubbles.

Pour to ½ inch high in a 4- to 6-cup ring or heart mold:

Cold distilled water

Freeze until almost completely frozen, then arrange in the mold and press gently into the ice:

Fresh strawberries or raspberries
Fresh mint leaves

Add enough additional distilled water to come about halfway up the sides of the berries but not enough to float them. Freeze until the berries and mint are frozen into position. Then add enough water to completely cover the berries and mint and freeze.

When ready to serve, dip the bottom of the mold into cold water for a few moments and invert onto a plate. Slide the ice ring from the plate into a punch bowl to float.

Cold Duck

10 servings

Inferior, semisweet sparkling red wine packaged under this name was something of a fad in America in the 1970s, perhaps ruining the name forever for some drinkers. But the original Cold Duck was a perfectly respectable wine-based drink and worthy of renewed consideration. (The curious name, incidentally, is a direct translation of the German Kalte Ente—*which in turn was probably a play on* Kalte Ende, *meaning something like cold leftovers.)*

In a 2-quart pitcher, place:

Zest of 1 lemon, removed in a single long spiral

Add:

2 jiggers (3 ounces) curaçao
1 bottle (750 ml) chilled semidry German or California Riesling
1 bottle (750 ml) chilled dry German or California sparkling wine

Serve in chilled wine glasses or champagne flutes.

Sangria

8 servings

Like two other Spanish classics, paella and gazpacho, sangria has achieved worldwide renown. Like these two dishes, sangria now exists in countless variations, most of them very far removed from the simplicity and savor of the original. Above all, remember two things about sangria: It is best made with dry, earthy-tasting Spanish red wine (an inexpensive Rioja, for instance), and it is not a fruit salad. When blood oranges are available, they make an attractive substitute for the more conventional navel oranges. Look for the Moro, Sanguinelli, or Tarocco varieties.

Combine in a 2- to 3-quart pitcher:

2 bottles (750 ml each) dry Spanish red wine

1 jigger (1½ ounces) Spanish brandy

2 jiggers (3 ounces) curaçao or Cointreau

Juice of 3 lemons

2 tablespoons *Sugar Syrup*, 110

3 oranges, thinly sliced

2 lemons, thinly sliced

Cover the pitcher with plastic wrap and allow the flavors to marry in the refrigerator for 5 to 6 hours.

Cooked Eggnog

18 servings

Do not double this recipe.
Combine and set aside:

1 cup milk
1 cup heavy cream

Whisk just until blended:

12 large egg yolks
1⅓ cups sugar
1 teaspoon freshly grated or ground nutmeg

Whisk in:

2 cups milk
2 cups heavy cream

Transfer to a large, heavy saucepan and place over low heat, stirring constantly, until the mixture becomes a little thicker than heavy cream (about 175°F). Do not overheat, or the mixture will curdle. Remove from the heat and immediately stir in the reserved milk and cream. Pour through a strainer. Chill thoroughly, uncovered, then stir in:

1½ cups brandy, Cognac, dark rum, or bourbon

Cover and refrigerate for at least 3 hours or up to 3 days. Serve sprinkled with:

Freshly grated or ground nutmeg

Glögg

20 servings

Glögg, the traditional Swedish spiced Christmas drink, was originally Mulled Wine (see opposite), *but over the years it came to acquire a considerably stronger alcoholic kick. Swedes often make it with high-proof neutral alcohol— a kind of personal antifreeze for icy Scandinavian winter nights—but brandy and aquavit or vodka give it a nice flavor.*
Combine in a large nonaluminum pot:

2 bottles (750 ml each) tawny port
1 bottle (750 ml) brandy
2 cups aquavit or vodka
Peel of 1 orange, cut in strips
1 cup raisins

Wrap securely in a small square of cheesecloth:

Four 3-inch cinnamon sticks
10 cloves
10 cardamom pods

Add to the pot, cover, and bring almost to a boil. Reduce the heat to low and simmer for 1 hour. Discard the spice package and orange zest. Holding the cover against the edge of the pot as a shield, hold a lighted long match near the rim of the pot until the alcohol fumes ignite. Let burn for 4 to 5 seconds, then extinguish by covering the pot. Ladle the glögg into warmed cups. Serve with small spoons for the raisins.

Wassail

20 servings

The name wassail comes from an old Norse toast meaning "Your health!" So healthy did this beverage make the old Norse feel that wassail came to mean not just a drink but the revelry it inspired. Wassail can also be made with a combination of beer and wine, preferably sherry, in which case the proportion could be roughly 4 parts beer to 1 part sherry. The baked apples flavor the wassail and add flare to its presentation.

Prepare and set aside *Baked Apples, below.*

Meanwhile, combine in a saucepan and boil for 5 minutes:

1 cup water
4 cups sugar
1 tablespoon ground nutmeg
2 teaspoons ground ginger
½ teaspoon ground mace
6 whole cloves
6 allspice berries
One 3-inch stick cinnamon

In a large bowl, beat until stiff but not dry:

12 large egg whites

In another large bowl, beat until light in color:

12 large egg yolks

Fold the whites into the yolks. Strain the sugar and spice mixture into the eggs, stirring quickly to combine. Bring almost to the boiling point in two separate saucepans:

4 bottles (750 ml each) sherry
  or Madeira
2 cups brandy

Slowly pour the hot wine into the spice and egg mixture, stirring briskly. Toward the end of this process, add the brandy. Just before serving and while the mixture is still foaming, add the *Baked Apples.*

Mulled Cider

4 servings

This satisfying alternative to Mulled Wine (right), is particularly good during the fall holiday season. A pleasant nonalcoholic version can be made by omitting the rum.

Combine in a saucepan:

2 jiggers (3 ounces) light or
  dark rum
1 bottle (750 ml) clear
  nonalcoholic apple cider
Four 3-inch cinnamon sticks
Peel of 1 orange, cut into 4 pieces,
  or 1 small navel orange, thinly
  sliced crosswise
1 tablespoon sugar

Simmer, covered, over low heat for 20 to 30 minutes to allow the flavors to blend. Ladle into warmed mugs, placing a cinnamon stick and a piece of orange peel or an orange slice in each mug.

Mulled Wine

4 servings

To make Vin Brûlé, a French variation on mulled wine, bring the same ingredients to a boil over high heat, then uncover and carefully ignite with a lighted long match. When the flames have died, ladle the wine into warmed mugs, garnishing them as directed. The French say this drink is better than aspirin to ward off a cold.

Combine in a saucepan:

1 bottle (750 ml) California
  Merlot or other dry red wine
Four 3-inch cinnamon sticks
Peel of 1 orange, cut into 4 pieces,
  or 1 small orange, thinly sliced
3 to 4 tablespoons sugar

Simmer, covered, over low heat for 20 to 30 minutes. Ladle into warmed mugs, placing a cinnamon stick and a piece of orange peel or an orange slice in each mug.

Baked Apples

For best results, choose a variety of apple that is firm, tart, and full of character.

Preheat oven to 350°F.

Core through the top, stopping ½ inch from the bottom:

12 small, firm, tart apples, such as
  Rome Beauty, McIntosh, Jonagold, or
  Granny Smith

Set the apples in a shallow 2- to 3-quart baking dish, just large enough to hold them without touching.

Combine:

⅔ cup packed brown sugar
Grated zest of 1 lemon
1 teaspoon ground nutmeg
½ teaspoon ground cinnamon

Spoon the mixture into the apples and scatter any that is left into the pan. Dot on top of the apples:

3 tablespoons unsalted butter, cut
  into small pieces

Pour into the pan:

1⅓ cups water or fresh sweet cider
  if available

Cover tightly with a lid or aluminum foil. Bake the apples for about 30 minutes. Uncover, baste with the syrup in the bottom of the pan, and bake until they are tender but not mushy, about 10 minutes more, depending on the variety.

Index

Bold type indicates that a recipe has an accompanying photograph.

Anchovy Toasts, 21
Angels on Horseback, 77
Apéritifs, 109
Apples, Baked, 125
Artichoke Dip, Baked, 24
Asparagus, Ham Rolls with, 92, 103
Avocados, 27
    Guacamole, 22, 29

Baba Ghanoush (Roasted Eggplant Dip), 30
Beans, 25
    Black, Salsa Dip, 25
    White, and Roasted Garlic Puree, 36
Beef
    Barbecued Kebabs, 96, 97
    Danish Sandwiches, 18
    Empanadas, 71
    Ground, Samosas with, 64
    Satay with Peanut Sauce, 94
    and Scallion Rolls (Negi Maki), 94, 95
    Swedish Meatballs, 97
Bellini, 121
Biscuits, 16–17
Black Russian, 115
Bloody Mary, 114
Blue Cheese
    Creamy Dressing, 84, 86
    Spread with Walnuts, 22, 36
Bocconcini (Marinated Mozzarella), 40
Brandy, 120
    Alexander, 120
Breads, yeast, 66
Bread Sticks with Serrano Ham, 103
Brie Baked in Pastry, 42
Bronx, 113
Bruschetta, 20, 21

Cabbage, Chinese, 72
Caviar
    Eggplant, 33
    New Potatoes Stuffed with, 53
Celery, Stuffed, 51
Champagne
    Cocktail, 121
    Punch, 122
Charcoal, 99
Cheese
    Fondue, 41
    Liptauer, 37

New Potatoes Stuffed with Bacon and, 52
    Puffs (Gougères), 56, 59
    Straws, 56, 60
    see also specific cheeses
Cheesecake, Pesto, 44, 45
Chicken, 89
    Dumplings, 90, 91
    Fingers, 84, 89
    Lemon Rosemary, on Skewers, 87
    Liver Pâté, 88
    Rumaki, 100, 101
    Wings, 86–87
Chickpea and Sesame Dip (Hummus), 30
Choux Paste, 58
Choux Puffs with Lobster Salad, 59
Chutney, Mint-Cilantro, 52
Cider, Mulled, 125
Clams Casino, 76
Cocktail Sauce, 78
Cold Duck, 122
Cordials, 121
Crab Dip, 25
Crackers, 16
Cranberry Collins, 115
Cream-Cheese Chutney Spread, 37
Crudités, 50
Cuba Libre, 117

Daiquiri, 116
Dips, 23–30, 37
Dumplings
    Chicken, 90, 91
    Chinese, 72

Eggnog, Cooked, 124
Eggplant
    Caviar, 33
    Roasted Dip (Baba Ghanoush), 30
Eggs
    Potato Omelet (Tortilla Española), 46, 54
    and Smoked Salmon Sandwiches, 18
Empanadas, 71

Fennel Wrapped in Prosciutto, 51
Feta
    and Spinach Triangles, 63
    Whipped, with Roasted Peppers, 36
Figs
    Bruschetta with Prosciutto and, 21
    and Melon Wrapped in Prosciutto, 48, 49
    Sausages with, 101

Fish Roe (Taramasalata), 22, 34
Five-spice powder, 98
Fondue, Cheese, 41
French 75, 120
Fruits, dried, 42
Fuzzy Navel, 121

Gimlet, 112, 113
Gin, 112
    Fizz, 112, 113
Glögg, 124
Goat Cheese
    with Cracked Pepper, 40
    Marinated, with Fresh Thyme, 40
Gougères (Cheese Puffs), 56, 59
Grape Leaves, Stuffed, 92, 105
Grasshopper, 121
Guacamole, 22, 29

Ham
    Biscuits, 16
    Rolls, with Asparagus, 92, 103
    Serrano, Bread Sticks with, 103
Harissa, 104
Herbs, 105
Hummus (Chickpea and Sesame Dip), 30

Ice Ring, Decorative, 122

Kielbasa in Quilts, 102
Kir, 121

Laban, Herbed (Yogurt Cheese), 43
Lamb
    Barbecued Kebabs, 96, 97
    Brochettes, 104
    Stuffed Grape Leaves, 92, 105
Lemon
    Crackers, 16
    Rosemary Chicken on Skewers, 87
Liptauer Cheese, 37
Lobster Salad, Choux Puffs with, 59

Mai Tai, 116
Mangoes, 81
    Salsa, 29
    and Shrimp Skewers, Molasses-Glazed, 81
Manhattan, 119
Margarita, 118
Martini, 106, 112

Masa Boats, 68, 69
Mayonnaise
    Blender, 78
    Garlic, 50
Meatballs, Swedish, 97
Melon and Figs Wrapped in Prosciutto, 48, 49
Menus, 11
Mimosa, 121
Mint Julep, 119
Miso, 91
Moscow Mule, 114
Mozzarella
    Bruschetta with Oregano and, 21
    Marinated (Bocconcini), 40
Mushrooms, 55, 62
    Portobello, Bruschetta with, 21
    Stuffed, 55
    Triangles, 62

Nachos, 15
Negi Maki (Beef and Scallion Rolls), 94, 95
Negroni, 113
Nuts, toasting, 36

Old-Fashioned, 119
Olive oils, extra-virgin, 101
Olives, 51
    Marinated, 51
    Small Pastries, 65
    Tapenade, 32
Onion Dip, 24
Oysters, 77
    Angels on Horseback, 77
    Rockefeller, 77

Parmesan Straws, 56, 60
Pastry, 42, 57–73
Pâté, Chicken Liver, 88
Peaches, Grilled with Balsamic Glaze, 48
Peanuts
    Dipping Sauce, 82, 84
    Sauce, Beef Satay with, 94
Peas, Samosas with Potatoes and, 64
Peppers
    Roasted, Whipped Feta with, 36
    stove-roasting, 18
Pesto
    Cheesecake, 44, 45
    Sauce, 44
Phyllo, 62–65
Pigs in a Blanket, 102

Piña Colada, 117
Pirozhki, 66, 67
Planter's Punch, 117
Pork
    Baby Riblets, 99
    Chinese Dumplings, 72
    Fried Wontons, 73
    Grilled Five-Spice Ribs, 98
    Swedish Meatballs, 97
Potatoes, 54
    Chips, 14
    New, Stuffed, 52, 53
    Omelet (Tortilla Española), 46, 54
    Patties, 52
    Samosas with Peas and, 64
    Skins, 52
Prosciutto
    Bruschetta with Figs and, 21
    Fennel Wrapped in, 51
    Melon and Figs Wrapped in, 48, 49
Puff Pastry, 61
Punch, Champagne, 122

Quesadillas, Griddle-Baked, 18, 19
Queso añejo, 69

Raita (Indian Yogurt Salad), 97
Rémoulade Sauce, 80
Root Chips, 13, 15
Rum, 116
    Hot Buttered, 117
Rumaki, 100, 101
Rusty Nail, 119

Salami Rolls, 103
Salmon
    Mousse, 34, 35
    Smoked, and Egg Sandwiches, 18
Salsas, 28–29
Salty Dog, 115
Samosas, 64
Sandwiches, 13, 18
Sangria, 123
Sauces
    Cocktail, 78
    Honey-Mustard Dipping, 84, 103
    Peanut Dipping, 82, 84
    Pesto, 44
    Rémoulade, 80
    Tartar, 78
Sausages
    with Figs, 101
    Kielbasa in Quilts, 102

    Mushrooms Stuffed with, 55
Sazerac, 119
Screwdriver, 115
Seven-Layer Dip, 27
Shirley Temple, 115
Shrimp
    Baked Honey, 80
    Beer-Batter, 80
    Cajun Popcorn, 81
    Danish Sandwiches, 18
    and Mango Skewers, 81
    No-Fail Boiled, 78, 79
    Vietnamese Summer Rolls, 82, 83
Sidecar, 120
Singapore Sling, 112, 113
Spinach
    and Feta Triangles, 63
    Yogurt Dip, 26
Spreads, 32–37
Stinger, 120
Sugar Syrup, 110
Summer Rolls, Vietnamese, 82, 83

Tapenade, 32
Taramasalata (Fish Roe), 22, 34
Tartar Sauce, 78
Tequila, 118
    Sunrise, 118
Tomatoes, Bruschetta with, 20
Tom Collins, 113
Tortilla Chips, 15
Tortilla Española (Potato Omelet), 46, 54
Trout Canapés, 74, 82
Tuna Tapenade, 32
Turkey Biscuits with Chutney Butter, 17

Vodka, 114

Wassail, 125
Water bath, 44
Water Chestnut Rumaki, 101
Whiskey, 119
    Sour, 119
Wine, 121
    Cocktails, 121
    Mulled, 125
    Spritzer, 121
Wontons, Fried, 73

Yogurt
    Cheese (Laban), 43
    Indian Salad (Raita), 97
    Spinach Dip, 26

Acknowledgments

Special thanks to my wife and editor in residence, Susan; our friend and editorial assistant, Cynthia Hoskin; and our friends and agents, Gene Winick and Sam Pinkus. Much appreciation also goes to Simon & Schuster, Scribner, and Weldon Owen for their devotion to this project. Thank you Carolyn, Susan, Beth, Rica, Bill, Marah, John, Terry, Roger, Gaye, Val, Norman, and all the other capable and talented folks who gave a part of themselves to the Joy of Cooking All About series.

My eternal appreciation goes to the food experts, writers, and editors whose contributions and collaborations are at the heart of Joy—especially Stephen Schmidt. He was to the 1997 edition what Chef Pierre Adrian was to Mom's final editions of Joy. Thank you one and all.

Ethan Becker

FOOD EXPERTS, WRITERS, AND EDITORS
Selma Abrams, Jody Adams, Samia Ahad, Bruce Aidells, Katherine Alford, Deirdre Allen, Pam Anderson, Elizabeth Andoh, Phillip Andres, Alice Arndt, John Ash, Nancy Baggett, Rick and Deann Bayless, Lee E. Benning, Rose Levy Beranbaum, Brigit Legere Binns, Jack Bishop, Carole Bloom, Arthur Boehm, Ed Brown, JeanMarie Brownson, Larry Catanzaro, Val Cipollone, Polly Clingerman, Elaine Corn, Bruce Cost, Amy Cotler, Brian Crawley, Gail Damerow, Linda Dann, Deirdre Davis, Jane Spencer Davis, Erica De Mane, Susan Derecskey, Abigail Johnson Dodge, Jim Dodge, Aurora Esther, Michele Fagerroos, Eva Forson, Margaret Fox, Betty Fussell, Mary Gilbert, Darra Goldstein, Elaine Gonzalez, Dorie Greenspan, Maria Guarnaschelli, Helen Gustafson, Pat Haley, Gordon Hamersley, Melissa Hamilton, Jessica Harris, Hallie Harron, Nao Hauser, William Hay, Larry Hayden, Kate Hays, Marcella Hazan, Tim Healea, Janie Hibler, Lee Hofstetter, Paula Hogan, Rosemary Howe, Mike Hughes, Jennifer Humphries, Dana Jacobi, Stephen Johnson, Lynne Rossetto Kasper, Denis Kelly, Fran Kennedy, Johanne Killeen and George Germon, Shirley King, Maya Klein, Diane M. Kochilas, Phyllis Kohn, Aglaia Kremezi, Mildred Kroll, Loni Kuhn, Corby Kummer, Virginia Lawrence, Jill Leigh, Karen Levin, Lori Longbotham, Susan Hermann Loomis, Emily Luchetti, Stephanie Lyness, Karen MacNeil, Deborah Madison, Linda Marino, Kathleen McAndrews, Alice Medrich, Anne Mendelson, Lisa Montenegro, Cindy Mushet, Marion Nestle, Toby Oksman, Joyce O'Neill, Suzen O'Rourke, Russ Parsons, Holly Pearson, James Peterson, Marina Petrakos, Mary Placek, Maricel Presilla, Marion K. Pruitt, Adam Rapoport, Mardee Haidin Regan, Peter Reinhart, Sarah Anne Reynolds, Madge Rosenberg, Nicole Routhier, Jon Rowley, Nancy Ross Ryan, Chris Schlesinger, Stephen Schmidt, Lisa Schumacher, Marie Simmons, Nina Simonds, A. Cort Sinnes, Sue Spitler, Marah Stets, Molly Stevens, Christopher Stoye, Susan Stuck, Sylvia Thompson, Jean and Pierre Troisgros, Jill Van Cleave, Patricia Wells, Laurie Wenk, Caroline Wheaton, Jasper White, Jonathan White, Marilyn Wilkenson, Carla Williams, Virginia Willis, John Willoughby, Deborah Winson, Lisa Yockelson.

Weldon Owen wishes to thank the following people for their generous assistance and support in producing this book: Desne Ahlers, Brynn Breuner, Ken DellaPenta, Kyrie Forbes, Arin Hailey, and Norman Kolpas. The photographers wish to thank Champ DeMar, San Francisco; Caruso/Woods, Santa Barbara; Beau Rivage, Santa Barbara; Nancy White; RubyLane.com; and Chrome Works.